The Nice Valour by Thomas Middleton

or, The Passionate Madman

The Nice Valour was first published in the Beaumont and Fletcher Folio of 1647, but modern analysis of the work has now confirmed the authorship of Middleton either in its entirety or a significant revision of an earlier Fletcher play.

Thomas Middleton was born in London in April 1580 and baptised on 18th April.

Middleton was aged only five when his father died. His mother remarried but this unfortunately fell apart into a fifteen year legal dispute regarding the inheritance due Thomas and his younger sister.

By the time he left Oxford, at the turn of the Century, Middleton had and published Microcynicon: Six Snarling Satirese which was denounced by the Archbishop of Canterbury and publicly burned.

In the early years of the 17th century, Middleton wrote topical pamphlets. One – Penniless Parliament of Threadbare Poets was reprinted several times and the subject of a parliamentary inquiry.

These early years writing plays continued to attract controversy. His writing partnership with Thomas Dekker brought him into conflict with Ben Jonson and George Chapman in the so-called War of the Theatres.

His finest work with Dekker was undoubtedly The Roaring Girl, a biography of the notorious Mary Frith.

In the 1610s, Middleton began another playwriting partnership, this time with the actor William Rowley, producing another slew of plays including Wit at Several Weapons and A Fair Quarrel.

The ever adaptable Middleton seemed at ease working with others or by himself. His solo writing credits include the comic masterpiece, A Chaste Maid in Cheapside, in 1613.

In 1620 he was officially appointed as chronologer of the City of London, a post he held until his death.

The 1620s saw the production of his and Rowley's tragedy, and continual favourite, The Changeling, and of several other tragicomedies.

However in 1624, he reached a peak of notoriety when his dramatic allegory A Game at Chess was staged by the King's Men. Though Middleton's approach was strongly patriotic, the Privy Council silenced the play after only nine performances at the Globe theatre, having received a complaint from the Spanish ambassador.

What happened next is a mystery. It is the last play recorded as having being written by Middleton.

Thomas Middleton died at his home at Newington Butts in Southwark in the summer of 1627, and was buried on July 4th, in St Mary's churchyard which today survives as a public park in Elephant and Castle.

Index of Contents

Dramatis Personae
(in order of appearance)
The DUKE
SHAMONT
Four GENTLEMEN of the Chamber, the first named LA NOVE
LAPET
The LADY, sister to the Duke
Lapet's WIFE
The PASSIONATE LORD, kinsman to the Duke
A SERVANT to Shamont
A SOLDIER, brother to Shamont
A Lady disguised as CUPID
Six women MASQUERS
Two BROTHERS to the Cupid
A PRIEST
A HUNTSMAN
GALOSHIO, a clown
Two SERVANTS to the Lady
A SERVANT to the Duke
A GALLANT
A PLAIN FELLOW
BASE, the Passionate Lord's jester
A SERVANT to the Passionate Lord

POLTROT
MOULBAZON

THE PROLOGUE at the reviving of this play

It's grown in fashion of late in these days
To come and beg a sufferance to our plays;
Faith, gentlemen, our poet ever writ
Language so good, mix'd with such sprightly wit,
He made the theatre so sovereign
With his rare scenes, he scorn'd this crouching vein:
We stabb'd him with keen daggers when we pray'd
Him write a preface to a play well made.
He could not write these toys; 'twas easier far
To bring a felon to appear at th' bar,
So much he hated baseness, which this day,
His scenes will best convince you of in's play.

ACT I

SCENE I - The Palace

Enter **DUKE, SHAMONT**, and four **GENTLEMEN** including **LA NOVE**.

DUKE
Shamont, welcome; we have miss'd thee long,
Though absent but two days: I hope your sports
Answer'd your time and wishes.

SHAMONT
Very nobly, sir:
We found game worthy your delight, my lord,
It was so royal.

DUKE
I've enough to hear on't;
Prithee bestow 't upon me in discourse.

[They walk apart.

LA NOVE
What is this gentleman, coz? You are a courtier,
Therefore know all their insides.

SECOND GENTLEMAN

No farther than the taffety goes, good coz,
For the most part, which is indeed the best part
Of the most general inside. Marry, thus far
I can with boldness speak this one's man's character,
And upon honour pass it for a true one:
He has that strength of manly merit in him
That it exceeds his sovereign's power of gracing;
He's faithfully true to valour, that he hates
The man from Caesar's time, or farther off,
That ever took disgrace unreveng'd,
And if he chance to read his abject story,
He tears his memory out, and holds it virtuous
Not to let shame have so much life amongst us.
There is not such a curious piece of courage
Amongst man's fellowship, or one so jealous
Of honour's loss or reputation's glory:
There's so much perfect of his growing story.

LA NOVE
'Twould make one dote on virtue as you tell it.

SECOND GENTLEMAN
I ha' told it to much loss, believe it, coz.

THIRD GENTLEMAN
How the duke graces him! What is he, brother?

FOURTH GENTLEMAN
Do you not yet know him? A vainglorious coxcomb,
As proud as he that fell for't:
Set but aside his valour, no virtue,
Which is indeed not fit for any courtier;
And we his fellows are as good as he,
Perhaps as capable of favour too,
For one thing or another, if 'twere look'd into.
Give me a man, were I a sovereign now,
Has a good stroke at tennis, and a stiff one,
Can play at equinoctium with the line,
As even as the thirteenth of September,
When day and night lie in a scale together.
Or may I thrive as I deserve at billiards,
No otherwise at chess, or at primero?
These are the parts requir'd, why not advanc'd?

DUKE
Trust me, it was no less than excellent pleasure,
And I'm right glad 'twas thine. [To **GENTLEMEN**] How fares our kinsman?
Who can resolve us best?

LA NOVE

I can, my lord.

DUKE

There if I had a pity without bounds,
It might be all bestow'd. A man so lost
In the wild ways of passion, that he's sensible
Of naught but what torments him!

LA NOVE

True, my lord,
He runs through all the passions of mankind,
And shifts 'em strangely too: one while in love,
And that so violent, that for want of business
He'll court the very prentice of a laundress,
Though she have kib'd heels: and in's melancholy again,
He will not brook an empress, though thrice fairer
Than ever Maud was, or higher spirited
Than Cleopatra or your English countess.
Then on a sudden he's so merry again,
Out-laughs a waiting woman before her first child;
And in the turning of a hand, so angry
H'as almost beat the northern fellow blind,
That is for that use only: if that mood hold, my lord,
H'ad need of a fresh man; I'll undertake
He shall bruise three a month.

DUKE

I pity him dearly,
And let it be your charge, with his kind brother,
To see his moods observ'd; let every passion
Be fed ev'n to a surfeit, which in time
May breed a loathing: let him have enough
Of every object that his sense is rapt with.
And being once glutted, then the taste of folly
Will come into disrelish.

LA NOVE

I shall see
Your charge, my lord, most faithfully effected.

[Exit **DUKE** with the **THREE** other **GENTLEMEN**.

And how does noble Shamont?

SHAMONT

Never ill, man,

Until I hear of baseness, then I sicken;
I am the healthful'st man i' th' kingdom else.

[Enter **LAPET** and stands apart.

LA NOVE
Be arm'd then for a fit: here comes a fellow
Will make you sick at heart, if baseness do't.

SHAMONT
Let me be gone. What is he?

LA NOVE
Let me tell you first
It can be but a qualm; pray, stay it out, sir:
Come, y'ave borne more than this.

SHAMONT
Borne? Never anything
That was injurious.

LA NOVE
Ha, I am far from that!

SHAMONT
He looks as like a man as I have seen one.
What would you speak of him? Speak well, I prithee,
Even for humanity's cause.

LA NOVE
You'd have it truth though?

SHAMONT
What else, sir? I have no reason to wrong heav'n
To favour nature; let her bear her own shame
If she be faulty.

LA NOVE
Monstrous faulty there, sir.

SHAMONT
I'm ill at ease already.

LA NOVE
Pray bear up, sir.

SHAMONT
I prithee let me take him down with speed then,

Like a wild object that I would not look upon.

LA NOVE
Then thus: he's one that will endure as much
As can be laid upon him.

SHAMONT
That may be noble:
I'm kept too long from his acquaintance.

LA NOVE
Oh, sir,
Take heed of rash repentance; y'are too forward
To find out virtue where it never settled:
Take the particulars first of what he endures,
Videlicet, bastinadoes by the great—

SHAMONT
How!

LA NOVE
Thumps by the dozen, and your kicks by wholesale.

SHAMONT
No more of him.

LA NOVE
The twinges by the nostril he snuffs up,
And holds it the best remedy for sneezing.

SHAMONT
Away!

LA NOVE
H'as been thrice switz'd from seven a' clock till nine,
Yet with a cart-horse stomach fell to breakfast,
Forgetful of his smart.

SHAMONT
Nay, the disgrace on't;
There is no smart but that: base things are felt
More by their shames than hurts. [To **LAPET**] Sir, I know you not,
But that you live an injury to nature,
I'm heartily angry with you.

LAPET
Pray give your blow or kick, and be gone then,
For I ne'er saw you before, and indeed

Have nothing to say to you, for I know you not.

SHAMONT
Why, wouldst thou take a blow?

LAPET
I would not, sir,
Unless 'twere offer'd me, and if from an enemy,
I'd be loath to deny it from a stranger.

SHAMONT
What, a blow?
Endure a blow? And shall he live that gives it?

LAPET
Many a fair year. Why not, sir?

SHAMONT
Let me wonder!
As full a man to see too, and as perfect!
I prithee live not long!

LAPET
How!

SHAMONT
Let me entreat it:
Thou dost not know what wrong thou dost mankind
To walk so long here, not to die betimes.
Let me advise thee, while thou hast to live here,
Ev'n for man's honour's sake, take not a blow more.

LAPET
You should advise them not to strike me then, sir,
For I'll take none, I assure you, 'less they are given.

SHAMONT
How fain would I preserve man's form from shame
And cannot get it done! However, sir,
I charge thee live not long.

LAPET
This is worse than beating.

SHAMONT
Of what profession art thou, tell me, sir,
Besides a tailor, for I'll know the truth.

LAPET
A tailor! I'm as a good a gentleman,
Can show my arms and all.

SHAMONT
How black and blue they are!
Is that your manifestation? Upon pain
Of pounding thee to dust, assume not wrongfully
The name of gentleman, because I am one
That must not let thee live.

LAPET
I have done, I have done, sir.
If there be any harm, beshrew the herald;
I'm sure I ha' not been so long a gentleman
To make this anger: I have nothing nowhere
But what I dearly pay for.

SHAMONT
Groom, be gone!

[Exit **LAPET**.

I never was so heartsick yet of man.

[Enter **LADY**, the Duke's sister, and Lapet's **WIFE**.

LA NOVE
Here comes a cordial, sir, from t'other sex,
Able to make a dying face look cheerful.

SHAMONT
The blessedness of ladies!

LADY
Y'are well met, sir.

SHAMONT
The sight of you has put an evil from me
Whose breath was able to make virtue sicken.

LADY
I'm glad I came so fortunately. What was't, sir?

SHAMONT
A thing that takes a blow, lives and eats after it
In very good health; you ha' not seen the like, madam:
A monster worth your sixpence, lovely worth.

LADY
Speak low, sir; by all likelihoods, 'tis her husband
That now bestow'd a visitation on thee.
Farewell, sir.

[Exit.

SHAMONT
Husband! Is't possible that he has a wife?
Would any creature have him? 'Twas some forc'd match;
If he were not kick'd to th' church o' th' wedding day,
I'll never come at court. Can be no otherwise.
Perhaps he was rich. Speak, Mistress Lapet,
Was it not so?

WIFE
Nay, that's without all question.

SHAMONT
Oh ho, he would not want kickers enow then!
If you are wise, I much suspect your honesty,
For wisdom never fastens constantly
But upon merit. If you incline to fool,
You are alike unfit for his society;
Nay, if it were not boldness in the man
That honours you to advise you, troth, his company
Should not be frequent with you.

WIFE
'Tis good counsel, sir.

SHAMONT
Oh, I am so careful where I reverence,
So just to goodness and her precious purity,
I am as equally jealous and as fearful
That any undeserved stain might fall
Upon her sanctified whiteness, as of the sin
That comes by willfulness.

WIFE
Sir, I love your thoughts,
And honour you for your counsel and your care.

SHAMONT
We are your servants.

WIFE [Aside]

He's but a gentleman
O' th' chamber; he might have kiss'd me. Faith,
Where shall one find less courtesy than at court?
Say I have an undeserver to my husband,
That's ne'er the worse for him: well, strange-lipp'd man,
'Tis but a kiss lost, there'll more come again.

[Exit. Enter the **PASSIONATE LORD**, the Duke's kinsman, makes a congie or two to nothing.

LA NOVE
Look who comes here, sir; his love-fit's upon him:
I know it by that set smile and those congies.
How courteous he's to nothing, which indeed
Is the next kin to woman; only shadow's
The elder sister of the twain, because 'tis seen too.
See how it kisses the forefinger still,
Which is the last edition, and being come
So near the thumb, every cobbler has got it.

SHAMONT
What a ridiculous piece humanity
Here makes itself!

LA NOVE
Nay, good, give leave a little, sir,
Y'are so precise a manhood.

SHAMONT
It afflicts me
When I behold unseemliness in an image
So near the godhead; 'tis an injury
To glorious eternity.

LA NOVE
Pray use patience, sir.

PASSIONATE LORD [To **LA NOVE**]
I do confess it freely, precious lady,
And love's suit is so: the longer it hangs,
The worse it is; better cut off, sweet madam.
Oh, that same drawing-in your nether lip there
Foreshows no goodness, lady. Make you question on't?
Shame on me but I love you.

LA NOVE
Who is't, sir,
You are at all this pains for? May I know her?

PASSIONATE LORD
For thee, thou fairest yet the falsest woman
That ever broke man's heartstrings.

LA NOVE
How? How's this, sir?

PASSIONATE LORD
What, the old trick of ladies? Man's apparel?
Will 't ne'er be left amongst you? Steal from court in't?

LA NOVE [Aside to **SHAMONT**]
I see the fit grows stronger.

PASSIONATE LORD
Pray let's talk a little.

SHAMONT [Aside to **LA NOVE**]
I can endure no more!

LA NOVE [Aside to **SHAMONT**]
Good, let us alone a little.
You are so exact a work: love light things somewhat, sir.

SHAMONT [Aside to **LA NOVE**]
Th'are all but shames.

LA NOVE
What is't you'd say to me, sir?

PASSIONATE LORD
Can you be so forgetful to enquire it, lady?

LA NOVE
Yes, truly, sir.

PASSIONATE LORD
The more I admire your flintiness.
What cause have I given you, illustrious madam,
To play this strange part with me?

LA NOVE
Cause enough;
Do but look back, sir, into your memory,
Your love to other women. Oh, lewd man,
'T 'as almost kill'd my heart! You see I'm chang'd with it;
I ha' lost the fashion of my sex with grief on't.
When I have seen you courting of a dowdy,

Compar'd with me, and kissing your forefinger
To one o' th' blackguards' mistresses: would not this
Crack a poor lady's heart that believ'd love
And waited for the comfort? But 'twas said, sir,
A lady of my hair cannot want pitying.
The country's coming up; farewell to you, sir.

PASSIONATE LORD
Whither intend you, sir?

LA NOVE
A long journey, sir:
The truth is, I'm with child and go to travel.

PASSIONATE LORD
With child? I never got it.

LA NOVE
I heard you were busy
At the same time, sir, and was loath to trouble you.

PASSIONATE LORD
Why, are not you a whore then, excellent madam?

LA NOVE
Oh, by no means: 'twas done, sir, in the state
Of my belief in you, and that quits me;
It lies upon your falsehood.

PASSIONATE LORD
Does it so?
You shall not carry her though, sir; she's my contract.

SHAMONT
I prithee, thou four elements ill-brew'd,
Torment none but thyself! Away, I say,
Thou beast of passion, as the drunkard is
The beast of wine! Dishonour to thy making,
Thou man in fragments!

PASSIONATE LORD
Hear me, precious madam.

SHAMONT [Aside]
Kneel for thy wits to heaven.

PASSIONATE LORD
Lady, I'll father it,

Whoe'er begot it: 'tis the course of greatness.

SHAMONT [Aside]
How virtue groans at this!

PASSIONATE LORD
I'll raise the court,
But I'll stay your flight.

[Exit.

SHAMONT
How wretched is that piece!

LA NOVE
He's the duke's kinsman, sir.

SHAMONT
That cannot take a passion away, sir,
Nor cut a fit but one poor hour shorter;
He must endure as much as the poorest beggar
That cannot change his money: there's the equality
In our impartial essence.

[Enter a **SERVANT**.

What's the news now?

SERVANT
Your worthy brother, sir, has left his charge
And come to see you.

[Enter Shamont's brother, a **SOLDIER**.

SHAMONT [Embracing him]
Oh, the noblest welcome
That ever came from man meet thy deservings!
Methinks I've all joy's treasure in mine arms now.

SOLDIER
You are so fortunate in prevention, brother,
You always leave the answerer barren, sir;
You comprehend in few words so much worth.

SHAMONT
'Tis all too little for thee; come, th'art welcome,
So I include all. Take especial knowledge, pray,
Of this dear gentleman, my absolute friend,

That loves a soldier far above a mistress,
Though excellently faithful to 'em both:
But love to manhood owns the purer troth.

[Exeunt.

SCENE I - A Gallery in the Palace

Enter Shamont's brother, a **SOLDIER**, and a **LADY**, the Duke's sister.

LADY
There should be in this gallery—Oh, th'are here.
Pray sit down; believe me, sir, I'm weary.

SOLDIER
It well becomes a lady to complain a little
Of what she never feels. Your walk was short, madam:
You can be but afraid of weariness,
Which well implies the softness of your sex;
As for the thing itself, you never came to't.

LADY
Y'are wondrously well read in ladies, sir.

SOLDIER
Shall I think such a creature as you, madam,
Was ever born to feel pain but in travail?
There's your full portion, besides a little toothache
In the breeding, which a kind husband too
Takes from you, madam.

LADY
But where do ladies, sir,
Find such kind husbands? Perhaps you have heard
The rheumatic story of some loving chandler now,
Or some such melting fellow, that you talk
So prodigal of men's kindness: I confess, sir,
Many of those wives are happy; their ambition
Does reach no higher than to love and ignorance,
Which makes an excellent husband, and a fond one.
Now, sir, your great ones aim at height and cunning,
And so are oft deceiv'd, yet they must venture it,
For 'tis a lady's contumely, sir,
To have a lord an ignorant; then the world's voice

Will deem her for a wanton ere she taste on't:
But to deceive a wise man, to whose circumspection
The world resigns itself with all his envy,
'Tis less dishonour to us then to fall
Because his believ'd wisdom keeps out all.

SOLDIER
Would I were the man, lady, that should venture
His wisdom to your goodness.

LADY
You might fail
In the return, as many men have done, sir.
I dare not justify what is to come of me,
Because I know it not, though I hope virtuously;
Marry, what's past or present, I durst put
Into a good man's hand, which if he take
Upon my word for good, it shall not cozen him.

SOLDIER
No, nor hereafter?

LADY
It may hap so too, sir.
A woman's goodness, when she is a wife,
Lies much upon a man's desert, believe it, sir;
If there be fault in her, I'll pawn my life on't,
'Tis first in him, if she were ever good,
That makes one. Knowing not a husband yet,
Or what he may be, I promise no more virtues
Than I may well perform, for that were cozenage.

SOLDIER
Happy were he that had you with all fears,
That's my opinion, lady.

[Enter **SHAMONT** and a **SERVANT** list'ning. They remain hidden and talk apart.

SERVANT
What say you now, sir?
Dare you give confidence to your own eyes?

SHAMONT
Not yet I dare not.

SERVANT
No?

SHAMONT
Scarce yet, or yet,
Although I see 'tis he. Why can a thing
That's but myself divided be so false?

SERVANT
Nay, do but mark how the chair plays his part too:
How amorously 'tis bent!

SHAMONT
Hell take thy bad thoughts,
For they are strange ones; never take delight
To make a torment worse! Look on 'em, heaven,
For that's a brother: send me a fair enemy
And take him, for a fouler fiend there breathes not.
I will not sin to think there's ill in her
But what's of his producing;
Yet goodness, whose enclosure is but flesh,
Holds out oft times but sorrily, but as black, sir,
As ever kindred was: I hate mine own blood,
Because it is so near thine. Live without honesty,
And mayst thou die with an unmoist'ned eye,
And no tear follow thee.

[Exeunt **SHAMONT, SERVANT.**

LADY
Y'are wondrous merry, sir;
I would your brother heard you.

SOLDIER
Or my sister;
I would not out o' th' way let fall my words, lady,
For the precisest humour.

[Enter **PASSIONATE LORD.**

PASSIONATE LORD [Aside]
Yea, so close?

SOLDIER
Th'are merry, that's the worst you can report on 'em;
Th'are neither dangerous nor immodest.

PASSIONATE LORD
So, sir,
Shall I believe you, think you?

SOLDIER
Who's this, lady?

LADY
Oh, the duke's cousin; he came late from travel, sir.

SOLDIER
Respect belongs to him.

PASSIONATE LORD
For as I said, lady,
Th'are merry, that's the worst you can report of 'em;
Th'are neither dangerous nor immodest.

SOLDIER
How's this?

PASSIONATE LORD
And there I think I left.

SOLDIER
Abuses me!

PASSIONATE LORD
Now to proceed, lady: perhaps I swore I lov'd you;
If you believe me not, y'are much the wiser.

SOLDIER
He speaks still in my person and derides me!

PASSIONATE LORD
For I can cog with you.

LADY
You can all do so:
We make no question of men's promptness that way.

PASSIONATE LORD
And smile, and wave a chair with comely grace too,
Play with our tassel gently, and do fine things
That catch a lady sooner than a virtue.

SOLDIER
I never us'd to let man live so long
That wrong'd me!

PASSIONATE LORD
Talk of battalions, woo you in a skirmish;

Divine my mind to you, lady, and being sharp set,
Can court you at half-pike, or name your weapon,
We cannot fail you, lady.

[Enter First Gentleman **LA NOVE**.

SOLDIER [Drawing his sword]
Now he dies!
Were all succeeding hopes stor'd up within him.

LA NOVE
Oh, fie! I' th' court, sir?

SOLDIER
I most dearly thank you, sir.

[He puts up his sword.

LA NOVE
'Tis rage ill spent upon a passionate madman.

SOLDIER
That shall not privilege him forever, sir.
A madman call you him? I have found too much reason
Sound in his injury to me to believe him so.

LA NOVE
If ever truth from man's lips may be held
In reputation with you, give this confidence,
And this his love-fit, which we observe still,
By's flattering and his fineness: at some other time,
He'll go as slovenly as heart can wish.
The love and pity that his highness shows to him
Makes every man the more respectful of him.
H'as never a passion but is well provided for;
As this of love, he is full fed in all,
His swinge as I may term it. Have but patience,
And ye shall witness somewhat.

SOLDIER
Still he mocks me,
Look you, in action, in behaviour, sir!
Hold still the chair, with a grand mischief to you,
Or I'll set so much strength upon your heart, sir!

PASSIONATE LORD
I feel some power has restrain'd me, lady:
If it be sent from love, say, I obey it,

And ever keep a voice to welcome it.

Song.
Thou deity, swift-winged love,
Sometimes below, sometimes above,
Little in shape, but great in power,
Thou that makest a heart thy tower,
And thy loopholes, ladies' eyes,
From whence thou strik'st the fond and wise:
Did all the shafts in thy fair quiver
Stick fast in my ambitious liver,
Yet thy power would I adore,
And call upon thee to shoot more.
Shoot more, shoot more.

[Enter a **LADY** like a Cupid off'ring to shoot at him.

I prithee hold, thou sweet, celestial boy;
I'm not requited yet with love enough
For the first arrow that I have within me:
And if thou be an equal archer, Cupid,
Shoot this lady and twenty more for me.

LADY
Me, sir?

LA NOVE [Aside to her]
'Tis nothing but device, fear it not, lady;
You may be as good a maid after that shaft, madam,
As e'er your mother was at twelve and a half:
'Tis like the boy that draws it, 't 'as no sting yet.

CUPID [Aside]
'Tis like the miserable maid that draws it
That sees no comfort yet, seeing him so passionate.

PASSIONATE LORD
Strike me the Duchess of Valois in love with me
With all the speed thou canst, and two of her women.

CUPID
You shall have more.

PASSIONATE LORD
Tell 'em I tarry for 'em.

[Exit **CUPID**.

LA NOVE [Aside to the **SOLDIER**]
Who would be angry with that walking trouble now
That hurts none but itself?

SOLDIER
I am better quieted.

PASSIONATE LORD
I'll have all womenkind struck in time for me
After thirteen once:
I see this Cupid will not let me want,
And let him spend his forty shafts an hour;
They shall be all found from the duke's exchequer.

[Enter again the same **CUPID**, her **TWO BROTHERS, SIX WOMEN MASQUERS**, Cupid's bow bent all the
way towards them, the first **WOMAN** singing and playing, a **PRIEST**.

He's come already.

The song.

FIRST WOMAN
Oh, turn thy bow,
Thy power we feel and know;
Fair Cupid, turn away thy bow:
They be those golden arrows
Bring ladies all their sorrows,
And till there be more truth in men,
Never shoot at maid again.

PASSIONATE LORD
What a felicity of whores are here!
And all my concubines struck bleeding new!
A man can in his lifetime make but one woman,
But he may make his fifty queans a month.

[The **CUPID** takes her **BROTHERS** and the **PRIEST** aside.]

CUPID
Have you rememb'red a priest, honest brothers?

FIRST BROTHER
Yes, sister, and this is the young gentleman;
Make you no question of our faithfulness.

SECOND BROTHER
This growing shame, sister, provokes our care.

PRIEST
He must be taken in this fit of love, gentlemen.

FIRST BROTHER
What else, sir? He shall do't.

SECOND BROTHER
Enough.

FIRST BROTHER
Be cheerful, wench.

[A dance, **CUPID** leading.

PASSIONATE LORD
Now by the stroke of pleasure, a deep oath.
Nimbly hopp'd, ladies all. What height they bear too!
A story higher than your common statures;
A little man must go upstairs to kiss 'em.
What a great space there is
Betwixt love's dining chamber and his garret!
I'll try the utmost height. The garret stoops methinks;
The rooms are made all bending, I see that,
And not so high as a man takes 'em for.

CUPID
Now if you'll follow me, sir, I've that power
To make them follow you.

PASSIONATE LORD
Are they all shot?

CUPID
All, all, sir, every mother's daughter of 'em.

PASSIONATE LORD
Then there's no fear of following; if they be
Once shot, they'll follow a man to th' devil.
As for you, sir—

[Exit with the **LADY**, the **CUPID**, the **BROTHERS**, the **PRIEST** and the **MASQUERS**.

SOLDIER
Me, sir?

LA NOVE
Nay, sweet sir.

SOLDIER
A noise, a threat'ning! Did you not hear it, sir?

LA NOVE
Without regard, sir, so would I have you.

SOLDIER
This must come to something: never talk of that, sir;
You never saw it otherwise.

LA NOVE
Nay, dear merit—

SOLDIER
Me, above all men!

LA NOVE
Troth, you wrong your anger.

SOLDIER
I will be arm'd, my honourable lecher—

LA NOVE
Oh, fie, sweet sir!

SOLDIER
That devours women's honesties by lumps
And never chaw'st thy pleasure.

LA NOVE
What do you mean, sir?

SOLDIER
What, does he mean t' engross all to himself?
There's others love a whore as well as he, sir.

LA NOVE
Oh, an' that be part o' th' fury, we have a city
Is very well provided for that case.
Let him alone with her, sir; we have women
Are very charitable to proper men,
And to a soldier that has all his limbs.
Marry, the sick and lame gets not a penny:
Right women's charity, and the husbands
Follow 't too.

[Enter **DUKE** and **LORDS** - the three other Gentlemen.

Here comes his highness, sir.

SOLDIER
I'll walk to cool myself.

[Exit.

DUKE
Who's that?

LA NOVE
The brother of Shamont.

DUKE
He's brother then
To all the court's love, they that love discreetly
And place their friendliness upon desert;
As for the rest, that with a double face
Look upon merit, much like fortune's visage,
That looks two ways, both to life's calms and storms,
I'll so provide for him, chiefly for him:
He shall not wish their loves nor dread their envies.

[Enter **SHAMONT**.

And here comes my Shamont.

SHAMONT [Aside]
That lady's virtues are my only joys,
And he to offer to lay siege to them!

DUKE
Shamont.

SHAMONT [Aside]
Her goodness is my pride; in all discourses,
As often as I hear rash-tongued gallants
Speak rudely of a woman, presently
I give in but her name and th'are all silent.
Oh, who would lose this benefit?

DUKE
Come hither, sir.

SHAMONT [Aside]
'Tis like the gift of healing but diviner,
For that but cures diseases in the body,
This works a cure on fame, on reputation,

The noblest piece of surgery upon earth.

DUKE
Shamont. He minds me not.

SHAMONT [Aside]
A brother do't?

DUKE
Shamont I say!

[Gives him a touch with his switch.

SHAMONT
Ha!

[Draws.

If he be mortal, by this hand he perishes!
Unless it be a stroke from heaven, he dies for't!

DUKE
Why, how now, sir? 'Twas I.

SHAMONT
The more's my misery.

DUKE
Why, what's the matter, prithee?

SHAMONT
Can you ask it, sir?
No man else should; stood forty lives before him,
By this I would have op'd my way to him.
It could not be you, sir; excuse him not,
Whate'er he be, as y'are dear to honour,
That I may find my peace again.

DUKE
Forbear, I say.
Upon my love to truth, 'twas none but I.

SHAMONT
Still miserable!

DUKE
Come, come, what ails you, sir?

SHAMONT
Never sat shame cooling so long upon me
Without a satisfaction in revenge,
And heaven has made it here a sin to wish it.

DUKE
Hark you, sir!

SHAMONT
Oh, y'ave undone me!

DUKE
How!

SHAMONT
Cruelly undone me;
I have lost my peace, and reputation by you:
Sir, pardon me, I can never love you more.

[Exit.

DUKE
What language call you this, sirs?

LA NOVE
Truth, my lord,
I've seldom heard a stranger.

SECOND GENTLEMAN
He is a man of a most curious valour,
Wondrous precise, and punctual in that virtue.

DUKE
But why to me so punctual? My last thought
Was most entirely fix'd on his advancement:
Why, I came now to put him in possession
Of his fair fortunes. What a misconceiver 'tis!
And from a gentleman of our chamber merely
Make him vice-admiral; I was settled in't.
I love him next to health. Call him, gentlemen.

[Exit **LA NOVE**.

Why, would not you or you ha' taken as much
And never murmur'd?

SECOND GENTLEMAN
Troth, I think we should, my lord,

And there's a fellow walks about the court
Would take a hundred of 'em.

DUKE
I hate you all for't,
And rather praise his high-pitch'd fortitude,
Though in extremes for niceness: now I think on't,
I would I had never done 't.

[Enter **LA NOVE**.

Now, sir, where is he?

LA NOVE
His suit is only, sir, to be excus'd.

DUKE
He shall not be excus'd, I love him dearlier:
Say we entreat him; go, he must not leave us.

[Exeunt **LA NOVE** and **SECOND GENTLEMAN**.

So virtue bless me, I ne'er knew him parallell'd;
Why, he's more precious to me now than ever.

[Enter **LA NOVE, SECOND GENTLEMAN** and **SHAMONT**.

SECOND GENTLEMAN
With much fair language, w'ave brought him.

DUKE
Thanks.
Where is he?

SECOND GENTLEMAN
Yonder, sir.

DUKE
Come forward, man.

SHAMONT
Pray pardon me, I'm asham'd to be seen, sir.

DUKE
Was ever such a touchy man heard of?
Prithee come nearer.

SHAMONT

More into the light?
Put not such cruelty into your requests, my lord,
First to disgrace me publicly, and then draw me
Into men's eyesight, with the shame yet hot
Upon my reputation.

DUKE
What disgrace, sir?

SHAMONT
What?
Such as there can be no forgiveness for
That I can find in honour.

DUKE
That's most strange, sir.

SHAMONT
Yet I have search'd my bosom to find one,
And wrestled with my inclination,
But 'twill not be: would you had kill'd me, sir,
With what an ease had I forgiven you then!
But to endure a stroke from any hand
Under a punishing angel's, which is justice,
Honour disclaim that man, for my part chiefly.
Had it been yet the malice of your sword,
Though it had cleft me, 't had been noble to me;
You should have found my thanks paid in a smile
If I had fell unworded: but to shame me
With the correction that your horse should have,
Were you ten thousand times my royal lord,
I cannot love you never, nor desire
To serve you more.
If your drum call me I am vowed to valour,
But peace shall never know me yours again,
Because I've lost mine own; I speak to die, sir.
Would you were gracious that way to take off shame,
With the same swiftness as you pour it on:
And since it is not in the power of monarchs
To make a gentleman, which is a substance
Only begot of merit, they should be careful
Not to destroy the worth of one so rare,
Which neither they can make nor lost, repair.

[Exit.

DUKE
Y'ave set a fair light, sir, before my judgment,

Which burns with wondrous clearness; I acknowledge it,
And your worth with it: but then, sir, my love,
My love— What, gone again?

LA NOVE
And full of scorn, my lord.

DUKE
That language will undo the man that keeps it
Who knows no difference 'twixt contempt and manhood.
Upon your love to goodness, gentlemen,
Let me not lose him long.

[Enter a **HUNTSMAN**.

How now?

HUNTSMAN
The game's at height, my lord.

DUKE
Confound both thee and it: hence break it off;
He hates me brings me news of any pleasure.
I felt not such a conflict since I could
Distinguish betwixt worthiness and blood.

[Exeunt.

ACT III

SCENE I - The Palace

Enter the **TWO BROTHERS**, **LA NOVE**, with those that were the **MASQUERS**, and the **CUPID**.

LA NOVE
I heartily commend your project, gentlemen;
'Twas wise and virtuous.

FIRST BROTHER
'Twas for the safety
Of precious honour, sir, which near blood binds us to:
He promis'd the poor easy fool there marriage;
There was a good maidenhead lost i 'th' belief on't,
Beshrew her hasty confidence.

LA NOVE

Oh, no more, sir,
You make her weep again! Alas, poor Cupid.
Shall she not shift herself?

FIRST BROTHER
Oh, by no means, sir.
We dare not have her seen yet; all the while
She keeps this shape, 'tis but thought device,
And she may follow him so without suspicion,
To see if she can draw all his wild passions,
To one point only, and that's love, the main point:
So far his highness grants, and gave at first,
Large approbation to the quick conceit,
Which then was quick indeed.

LA NOVE
You make her blush, in sooth.

FIRST BROTHER
I fear 'tis more the flag of shame than grace, sir.

LA NOVE
They both give but one kind of colour, sir:
If it be bashfulness in that kind taken,
It is the same with grace; and there she weeps again.
In truth y'are too hard, much, much too bitter, sir,
Unless you mean to have her weep her eyes out,
To play a Cupid truly.

FIRST BROTHER
Come, ha' done then:
We should all fear to sin first, for 'tis certain,
When 'tis once lodg'd, though entertain'd in mirth,
It must be wept out if it e'er come forth.

LA NOVE
Now 'tis so well, I'll leave you.

FIRST BROTHER
Faithfully welcome, sir.

[Exit **LA NOVE**.

Go, Cupid, to your charge; he's your own now:
If he want love, none will be blam'd but you.

CUPID [Aside]
The strangest marriage and unfortunat'st bride

That ever human memory contain'd;
I cannot be myself for't.

[Exit with **MASQUERS**. Enter **GALOSHIO** the clown.

GALOSHIO
Oh, gentlemen!

FIRST BROTHER
How now, sir, what's the matter?

GALOSHIO
His melancholy passion is half spent already, then comes his angry fit at the very tail on't, then comes in my pain, gentlemen; h'as beaten me e'en to a cullis. I am nothing, right worshipful, but very pap and jelly: I have no bones, my body's all one burstness. They talk of ribs and chines most freely abroad i' th' world; why, I have no such thing: whoever lives to see me dead, gentlemen, shall find me all mummy, good to fill gallipots and long dildo glasses; I shall not have a bone to throw at a dog.

BROTHERS
Alas, poor vassal, how he goes!

GALOSHIO
Oh, gentlemen,
I am unjointed, do but think o' that.
My breast is beat into my maw, that what I eat,
I am fain to take 't in all at mouth with spoons;
A lamentable hearing, and 'tis well known
My belly is driven into my back.
I earn'd four crowns a month most dearly, gentlemen,
And one he must have when the fit's upon him;
The privy purse allows it, and 'tis thriftiness:
He would break else some forty pounds in casements,
And in five hundred years undo the kingdom;
I have cast it up to a quarrel.

FIRST BROTHER
There's a fellow
Kick'd about court; I would he had his place, brother,
But for one fit of his indignation.

SECOND BROTHER
And suddenly I have thought upon a means for't.

FIRST BROTHER
I prithee, how?

SECOND BROTHER
'Tis but preferring, brother,

This stockfish to his service, with a letter
Of commendations, the same way he wishes it,
And then you win his heart, for o' my knowledge
He has laid wait this half-year for a fellow
That will be beaten; and with a safe conscience
We may commend the carriage of this man in't.
No servants he has kept—lusty, tall feeders—
But they have beat him and turn'd themselves away:
Now one that would endure is like to stay
And get good wages of him; and the service too
Is ten times milder, brother, I would not wish it else.
I see the fellow has a sore crush'd body,
And the more need he has to be kick'd at ease.

GALOSHIO
Ay, sweet gentlemen, a kick of ease;
Send me to such a master.

SECOND BROTHER
No more I say;
We have one for thee, a soft-footed master,
One that wears wool in's toes.

GALOSHIO
Oh, gentlemen,
Soft garments may you wear, soft skins may you wed,
But as plump as pillows, both for white and red!
And now will I reveal a secret to you,
Since you provide for my poor flesh so tenderly:
H'as hir'd mere rogues out of his chamber window
To beat the soldier, Monsieur Shamont's brother.

FIRST BROTHER
That nothing concerns us, sir.

GALOSHIO
For no cause, gentlemen,
Unless it be for wearing shoulder-points
With longer tags than his.

SECOND BROTHER
Is not that somewhat?
Birlakin, sir, the difference of long tags
Has cost many a man's life, and advanc'd other some.
Come, follow me.

GALOSHIO [Aside]
See what a gull am I!

Oh, every man in his profession!
I know a thump now, as judiciously
As the proudest he that walks, I'll except none.
Come to a tag, how short I fall! I'm gone.

[Exeunt.

SCENE II - The Palace

Enter **LAPET**.

LAPET
I have been ruminating with myself
What honour a man loses by a kick.
Why, what's a kick? The fury of a foot,
Whose indignation commonly is stamp'd
Upon the hinder quarter of a man,
Which is a place very unfit for honour;
The world will confess so much.
Then what disgrace I pray does that part suffer
Where honour never comes? I'd fain know that!
This being well-forc'd and urg'd may have the power
To move most gallants to take kicks in time,
And spurn out the duelloes out o' th' kingdom,
For they that stand upon their honour most,
When they conceive there is no honour lost,
As by a table that I have invented
For that purpose alone shall appear plainly,
Which shows the vanity of all blows at large,
And with what ease they may be took of all sides,
Numbering but twice o'er the letters "Patience"
From P. to E. I doubt not but in small time
To see a dissolution of all bloodshed
If the reform'd kick do but once get up,
For what a lamentable folly 'tis,
If we observe 't, for every little justle,
Which is but the ninth part of a sound thump
In our meek computation. We must fight forsooth, yes:
If I kill, I'm hang'd; if I be kill'd myself,
I die for't also. Is not this trim wisdom?
Now for the con: a man may be well-beaten,
Yet pass away his fourscore years smooth after;
I had a father did it, and to my power
I will not be behind him.

[Enter **SHAMONT**.

SHAMONT
Oh, well met.

LAPET [Aside]
Now a fine punch or two, I look for't duly.

SHAMONT
I've been to seek you.

LAPET
Let me know your lodging, sir,
I'll come to you once a day and use your pleasure, sir.

SHAMONT
I'm made the fittest man for thy society;
I'll live and die with thee. Come, show me a chamber;
There is no house but thine, but only thine,
That's fit to cover me: I've took a blow, sirrah.

LAPET
I would you had indeed; why, you may see, sir,
You'll all come to't in time when my book's out.

SHAMONT
Since I did see thee last, I've took a blow.

LAPET
Fa, sir, that's nothing; I ha' took forty since.

SHAMONT
What? And I charg'd thee thou shouldst not!

LAPET
Ay, sir,
You might charge your pleasure, but they would give 't me,
Whether I would or no.

SHAMONT
Oh, I walk
Without my peace, I've no companion now!
Prithee resolve me, for I cannot ask
A man more beaten to experience
Than thou art in this kind, what manner of blow
Is held the most disgraceful or distasteful?
For thou dost only censure 'em by the hurt,
Not by the shame they do thee: yet having felt
Abuses of all kinds, thou mayst deliver,

Though 't be by chance, the most injurious one.

LAPET
You put me to't, sir; but to tell you truth,
Th'are all as one with me, little exception.

SHAMONT
That little may do much; let's have it from you.

LAPET
With all the speed I may: first then and foremost,
I hold so reverently of the bastinado, sir,
That if it were the dearest friend i' th' world
I'd put it into his hand.

SHAMONT
Go to, I'll pass
That then.

LAPET
Y'are the more happy, sir; would I
Were past it too, but being accustom'd to't,
It is the better carried.

SHAMONT
Will you forward?

LAPET
Then there's your souse, your wherret, and your doust,
Tugs on the hair, your bob o' th' lips, a whelp on't:
I ne'er could find much difference. Now your thump,
A thing deriv'd first from your hemp-beaters,
Takes a man's wind away most spitefully:
There's nothing that destroys a colic like it,
For't leaves no wind i' th' body.

SHAMONT
On, sir, on.

LAPET
Pray give me leave; I'm out of breath with thinking on't.

SHAMONT
This is far off yet.

LAPET
For the twinge by th' nose,
'Tis certainly unsightly, so my table says,

But helps against the headache wondrous strangely.

SHAMONT
Is't possible?

LAPET
Oh, your crush'd nostrils slakes your oppilation
And makes your pent powers flush to wholesome sneezes.

SHAMONT
I never thought there had been half that virtue
In a wrung nose before.

LAPET
Oh, plenitude, sir:
Now come we lower to our modern kick,
Which has been mightily in use of late,
Since our young men drank coltsfoot: and I grant you,
'Tis a most scornful wrong, 'cause the foot plays it;
But mark again how we that take 't, requite it
With the like scorn, for we receive it backward,
And can there be a worse disgrace retorted?

SHAMONT
And is this all?

LAPET
All but a lug by th' ear,
Or such a trifle.

SHAMONT
Happy sufferer,
All this is nothing to the wrong I bear:
I see the worst disgrace thou never felt'st yet;
It is so far from thee, thou canst not think on't,
Nor dare I let thee know, it is so abject.

LAPET
I would you would though, that I might prepare for't,
For I shall ha't at one time or another:
If't be a thwack, I make account of that;
There's no new fashion'd swap that e'er came up yet
But I've the first on 'em, I thank 'em for't.

[Enter the **LADY** and **SERVANTS**.

LADY
Hast thou enquir'd?

FIRST SERVANT
But can hear nothing, madam.

SHAMONT [Aside to **LAPET**]
If there be but so much substance in thee
To make a shelter for a man disgrac'd,
Hide my departure from that glorious woman
That comes with all perfection about her,
So noble that I dare not be seen of her
Since shame took hold of me. Upon thy life
No mention of me.

LAPET [Aside to **SHAMONT**]
I'll cut out my tongue first
Before I'll lose my life, there's more belongs to't.

[Exit **SHAMONT**.

LADY
See, there's a gentleman: enquire of him.

SECOND SERVANT
For Monsieur Shamont, madam?

LADY
For whom else, sir?

FIRST SERVANT
Why, this fellow dares not see him.

LADY
How?

FIRST SERVANT
Shamont, madam?
His very name's worse than a fever to him,
And when he cries, there's nothing stills him sooner.
Madam, your page of thirteen is too hard for him;
'Twas try'd i' th' wood-yard.

LADY
Alas, poor, grieved merit!
What is become of him? If he once fail,
Virtue shall find small friendship. Farewell then
To ladies' worths for any hope in men:
He lov'd for goodness, not for wealth or lust,
After the world's foul dotage; he ne'er courted

The body but the beauty of the mind,
A thing which common courtship never thinks on.
All his affections were so sweet and fair;
There is no hope for fame if he despair.

[Exeunt **LADY** and **SERVANTS**. Enter **GALOSHIO** the clown. He kicks **LAPET** and gives him letter.

LAPET
Good morrow to you again most heartily, sir;
Cry you mercy I heard you not, I was somewhat busy.

GALOSHIO [Aside]
He takes it as familiarly as an ave
Or precious salutation: I was sick
Till I had one, because I am so us'd to't.

LAPET
However you deserve, your friends and mine here
Give you large commendations i' this letter;
They say you will endure well.

GALOSHIO
I'd be loath
To prove 'em liars: I've endur'd as much
As mortal pen and ink can set me down for.

LAPET
Say you me so?

GALOSHIO
I know and feel it so, sir:
I have it under black and white already;
I need no pen to paint me out.

LAPET [Aside]
He fits me,
And hits my wishes pat, pat: I was ne'er
In possibility to be better mann'd,
For he's half lam'd already; I see 't plain,
But take no notice on't for fear I make
The rascal proud and dear to advance his wages.—
First let me grow into particulars with you.
What have you endur'd of worth? Let me hear.

GALOSHIO
Marry, sir, I'm almost beaten blind.

LAPET

That's pretty well for a beginning,
But many a millhorse has endur'd as much.

GALOSHIO
Shame o' the miller's heart for his unkindness then.

LAPET
Well, sir, what then?

GALOSHIO
I've been twice thrown downstairs just before supper.

LAPET
Puh, so have I! That's nothing.

GALOSHIO
Ay, but, sir,
Was yours pray before supper?

LAPET
There thou posest me.

GALOSHIO
Ay, marry, that's it; 't 'ad been less grief to me
Had I but fill'd my belly and then tumbled,
But to be flung down fasting, there's the dolour.

LAPET
It would have griev'd me, that indeed. Proceed, sir.

GALOSHIO
I have been pluck'd and tugg'd by th' hair o' th' head
About a gallery, half an acre long.

LAPET
Yes, that's a good one, I must needs confess,
A principal good one that, an absolute good one;
I have been trod upon, and spurn'd about,
But never tugg'd by th' hair, I thank my fates.

GALOSHIO
Oh, 'tis a spiteful pain!

LAPET
Peace, never speak on't
For putting me in mind on't.

GALOSHIO

To conclude,
I'm bursten, sir: my belly will hold no meat.

LAPET
No? That makes amends for all.

GALOSHIO
Unless 't be puddings
Or such fast food: any loose thing beguiles me;
I'm ne'er the better for't.

LAPET
Sheepsheads will stay
With thee?

GALOSHIO
Yes, sir, or chaldrons.

LAPET
Very well, sir.
Any your bursten fellows must take heed of surfeits.
Strange things it seems you have endur'd.

GALOSHIO
Too true, sir.

LAPET
But now the question is, what you will endure
Hereafter in my service?

GALOSHIO
Anything
That shall be reason, sir, for I'm but froth;
Much like a thing new-calv'd, or come more nearer, sir,
Y'ave seen a cluster of frog-spawns in April:
E'en such a starch am I, as weak and tender
As a green woman yet.

LAPET
Now I know this,
I will be very gently angry with thee
And kick thee carefully.

GALOSHIO
Oh, ay, sweet sir!

LAPET
Peace, when thou art offer'd well, lest I begin now.

Your friends and mine have writ here for your truth;
They'll pass their words themselves and I must meet 'em.

GALOSHIO
Then have you all.

[Exit **LAPET**].

As for my honesty there is no fear of that,
For I have ne'er a whole bone about me.

[Exit.

SCENE III - The Passionate Lord's Chambers

Music. Enter the **PASSIONATE LORD**, rudely and carelessly apparell'd, unbrac'd and untruss'd, the **CUPID**
following.

CUPID
Think upon love, which makes all creatures handsome,
Seemly for eyesight; go not so diffusedly:
There are great ladies purpose, sir, to visit you.

PASSIONATE LORD
Grand plagues, shut in my casements, that the breaths
Of their coach-mares reek not into my nostrils;
Those beasts are but a kind of bawdy forerunners.

CUPID
It is not well with you when you speak ill of fair ladies.

PASSIONATE LORD
Fair mischiefs! Give me a nest of owls, and take 'em!
Happy is he, say I, whose window opens
To a brown baker's chimney: he shall be sure there
To hear the bird sometimes after twilight.
What a fine thing 'tis, methinks, to have our garments
Sit loose upon us thus, thus carelessly;
It is more manly and more mortifying,
For w'are so much the readier for our shrouds:
For how ridiculous were 't to have death come
And take a fellow pinn'd up like a mistress?
About his neck a ruff, like a pinch'd lanthorn,
Which schoolboys make in winter, and his doublet
So close and pent, as if he fear'd one prison
Would not be strong enough to keep his soul in,

But's tailor makes another?
An' trust me, for I know 't when I lov'd, Cupid,
He does endure much pain for the poor praise
Of a neat-sitting suit.

CUPID
One may be handsome, sir,
And yet not pain'd nor proud.

PASSIONATE LORD
There you lie, Cupid,
As bad as Mercury: there is no handsomeness
But has a wash of pride and luxury,
And you go there too, Cupid. Away, dissembler,
Thou tak'st the deed's part which befools us all;
Thy arrowheads shoot but sinners: hence, away,
And after thee I'll send a powerful charm
Shall banish thee forever.

CUPID
Never, never;
I am too sure thine own.

[Exit.

PASSIONATE LORD sings
Hence, all you vain delights,
As short as are the nights
Wherein you spend your folly,
There's naught in this life sweet,
If men were wise to see 't,
But only melancholy,
Oh, sweetest melancholy!
Welcome, folded arms and fixed eyes,
A sigh that piercing mortifies,
A look that's fast'ned to the ground,
A tongue chain'd up without a sound.
Fountainheads and pathless groves,
Places which pale passion loves,
Moonlight walks, when all the fowls
Are warmly hous'd save bats and owls;
A midnight bell, a parting groan,
These are the sounds we feed upon,
Then stretch our bones in a still gloomy valley:
Nothing's so dainty sweet as lovely melancholy.

[Exit.

Enter **LAPET**, at another door the Cupid's **BROTHERS** watching his coming and talking apart.

FIRST BROTHER
So, so, the woodcock's ginn'd; keep this door fast, brother.

SECOND BROTHER
I'll warrant this.

FIRST BROTHER
I'll go incense him instantly;
I know the way to't.

SECOND BROTHER
Will 't not be too soon,
Think you, and make two fits break into one?

FIRST BROTHER
Pah, no, no; the tail of his melancholy
Is always the head of his anger, and follows as close
As the report follows the powder.

[Exeunt the **BROTHERS** severally.

LAPET
This is the appointed place and the hour struck;
If I can get security for's truth,
I'll never mind his honesty. Poor worm,
I durst lay him by my wife, which is a benefit
Which many masters ha' not: I shall ha' no maid
Now got with child but what I get myself,
And that's no small felicity. In most places
Th'are got by th' men, and put upon the masters.
Nor shall I be resisted when I strike,
For he can hardly stand; these are great blessings.

PASSIONATE LORD [Within]
I want my food, deliver me a varlet!

LAPET
How now? From whence comes that?

PASSIONATE LORD [Within]
I am allow'd
A carcass to insult on. Where's the villain?

LAPET
He means not me, I hope.

PASSIONATE LORD [Within]
My maintenance, rascals!
My bulk, my exhibition!

LAPET
Bless us all,
What names are these? Would I were gone again.

[The **PASSIONATE LORD** enters in fury with a truncheon.

PASSIONATE LORD [sings]
A curse upon thee for a slave!
Art thou here and heard'st me rave?
Fly not sparkles from mine eye
To show my indignation nigh?
Am I not all foam and fire,
With voice as hoarse as a town-crier?
How my back opes and shuts together
With fury as old men's with weather!
Couldst thou not hear my teeth gnash hither?

LAPET
No, truly, sir, I thought 't had been a squirrel,
Shaving a hazelnut.

PASSIONATE LORD
Death, hell, fiends, and darkness,
I will thrash thy mangy carcass!

[Beats him.

LAPET
Oh, sweet sir!

PASSIONATE LORD
There cannot be too many tortures
Spent upon those lousy quarters!

LAPET
Hold, oh!

[Falls down for dead.

PASSIONATE LORD

Thy bones shall rue, thy bones shall rue!

[Sings again.

Thou nasty, scurvy, mongrel toad,
Mischief on thee!
Light upon thee
All the plagues that can confound thee
Or did ever reign abroad!
Better a thousand lives it cost
Than have brave anger spilt or lost.

[Exit.

LAPET
May I open mine eyes yet and safely peep?
I'll try a groan first. Oh! Nay, then he's gone.
There was no other policy but to die,
He would ha' made me else. Ribs, are you sore?
I was ne'er beaten to a tune before.

[Enter the **TWO BROTHERS**.

FIRST BROTHER
Lapet.

LAPET
Again?

[Falls again.

FIRST BROTHER
Look, look, he's flat again,
And stretched out like a corse, a handful longer
Than he walks, trust me, brother. Why, Lapet!
I hold my life we shall not get him speak now.
Monsieur Lapet? It must be a privy token
If anything fetch him, he's so far gone.
We come to pass our words for your man's truth.

LAPET
Oh, gentlemen, y'are welcome! I have been thrash'd, i'faith.

SECOND BROTHER
How! Thrash'd, sir?

LAPET
Never was Shrove Tuesday bird

So cudgell'd, gentlemen.

FIRST BROTHER
Pray how? By whom, sir?

LAPET
Nay, that I know not.

FIRST BROTHER
Not who did this wrong?

LAPET
Only a thing came like a walking song.

FIRST BROTHER
What, beaten with a song?

LAPET
Never more tightly, gentlemen.
Such crotchets happen now and then; methinks
He that endures well of all waters drinks.

[Exeunt.

ACT IV

SCENE I - A Chamber in the Palace, Outside the Palace, and in Front of Lapet's House

Enter Shamont's brother the **SOLDIER**, having been beaten, and **LA NOVE**.

SOLDIER
Yes, yes, this was a madman, sir, with you,
A passionate madman.

LA NOVE
Who would ha' look'd for this, sir?

SOLDIER
And must be privileg'd? A pox privilege him!
I was never so dry-beaten since I was born,
And by a litter of rogues, mere rogues, the whole twenty
Had not above nine elbows amongst 'em all too!
And the most part of those left-handed rascals
The very vomit, sir, of hospitals,
Bridewells and spitalhouses, such nasty smellers,
That if they'd been unfurnish'd of club-truncheons,
They might have cudgell'd me with their very stinks,

It was so strong and sturdy. And shall this,
This filthy injury, be set off with madness?

LA NOVE
Nay, take your own blood's counsel, sir; hereafter
I'll deal no further in't, if you remember
It was not come to blows when I advis'd you.

SOLDIER
No, but I ever said 'twould come to something,
And 'tis upon me, thank him: were he kin
To all the mighty emperors upon earth,
He has not now in life three hours to reckon;
I watch but a free time.

[Enter **SHAMONT**.

LA NOVE
Your noble brother, sir; I'll leave you now.

[Exit.

SHAMONT
Soldier, I would I could persuade my thoughts
From thinking thee a brother, as I can
My tongue from naming on't: thou hast no friend here
But fortune and thy own strength, trust to them.

SOLDIER
How? What's the incitement, sir?

SHAMONT
Treachery to virtue,
Thy treachery, thy faithless circumvention.
Has honour so few daughters, never fewer,
And must thou aim thy treachery at the best,
The very front of virtue, that bless'd lady,
The duke's sister?
Created more for admiration's cause
Than for love's ends, whose excellency sparkles
More in divinity than mortal beauty,
And as much difference 'twixt her mind and body
As 'twixt this earth's poor centre and the sun.
And couldst thou be so injurious to fair goodness,
Once to attempt to court her down to frailty?
Or put her but in mind that there is weakness,
Sin and desire, which she should never hear of?
Wretch, thou'st committed worse than sacrilege

In the attempting on't, and oughtst to die for't.

SOLDIER
I rather ought to do my best, to live, sir.
Provoke me not, for I've a wrong sits on me
That makes me apt for mischief; I shall lose
All respects suddenly of friendship, brotherhood,
Or any sound that way.

SHAMONT
But 'ware me most,
For I come with a two-edg'd injury,
Both my disgrace and thy apparent falsehood,
Which must be dangerous.

SOLDIER
I courted her, sir:
Love starve me with delays when I confess it not.

SHAMONT
There's nothing then but death
Can be a penance fit for that confession.

SOLDIER
But far from any vicious taint.

SHAMONT
Oh, sir,
Vice is a mighty stranger grown to courtship.

SOLDIER
Nay then, the fury of my wrong light on thee.

[They draw. Enter **LA NOVE** and the **THREE OTHER GENTLEMEN**.

LA NOVE
Forbear, the duke's at hand,
Here, hard at hand, upon my reputation.

SOLDIER
I must do something now.

[Exit **SOLDIER**.

SHAMONT
I'll follow you close, sir.

LA NOVE

We must entreat you must not, for the duke
Desires some conference with you.

SHAMONT
Let me go,
As y'are gentlemen.

SECOND GENTLEMAN
Faith, we dare not, sir.

SHAMONT
Dare ye be false to honour, and yet dare not
Do a man justice? Give me leave.

LA NOVE
Good, sweet sir,
H'as sent twice for you.

SHAMONT
Is this brave or manly?

LA NOVE
I prithee be conform'd.

SHAMONT
Death!

[Enter **DUKE**.

SECOND GENTLEMAN
Peace, he's come, in troth.

SHAMONT
Oh, have you betray'd me to my shame afresh?
How am I bound to loathe you!

DUKE
Shamont, welcome;
I sent twice.

SECOND GENTLEMAN
But, my lord, he never heard on't.

SHAMONT
Pray pardon him for his falseness. I did, sir,
Both times; I'd rather be found rude than faithless.

DUKE

I love that bluntness dearly: h'as no vice
But is more manly than some other's virtue,
That sets it out only for show or profit.

[Exeunt **LA NOVE** and the **THREE OTHER GENTLEMEN**.

SHAMONT
Will't please you quit me, sir? I've urgent business.

DUKE
Come, you're so hasty now: I sent for you
To a better end.

SHAMONT
And if it be an end,
Better or worse, I thank your goodness for't.

DUKE
I've ever kept that bounty in condition
And thankfulness in blood, which well becomes
Both prince and subject, that where any wrong
Bears my impression, or the hasty figure
Of my repented anger, I'm a law
Ev'n to myself, and doom myself most strictly
To justice and a noble satisfaction:
So that, what you in tenderness of honour
Conceive to be loss to you, which is nothing
But curious opinion, I'll restore again,
Although I give you the best part of Genoa,
And take to boot but thanks for your amends.

SHAMONT
Oh, miserable satisfaction,
Ten times more wretched than the wrong itself!
Never was ill better made good with worse.
Shall it be said that my posterity
Shall live the sole heirs of their father's shame,
And raise their wealth and glory from my stripes?
You have provided nobly bounteous, sir,
For my disgrace, to make it live forever,
Outlasting brass or marble;
This is my fear's construction, and a deep one,
Which neither argument nor time can alter:
Yet I durst swear I wrong your goodness in't, sir,
And the most fair intent on't, which I reverence
With admiration, that in you a prince
Should be so sweet and temperate a condition
To offer to restore where you may ruin,

And do't with justice, and in me a servant,
So harsh a disposition, that I cannot
Forgive where I should honour, and am bound to't.
But I have ever had that curiosity
In blood and tenderness of reputation,
Such an antipathy against a blow—
I cannot speak the rest. Good sir, discharge me;
It is not fit that I should serve you more,
Nor come so near you. I'm made now for privacy
And a retir'd condition; that's my suit,
To part from court forever, my last suit,
And as you profess bounty, grant me that, sir.

DUKE
I would deny thee nothing.

SHAMONT
Health reward you, sir.

[Exit.

DUKE
He's gone again already, and takes hold
Of any opportunity; not riches
Can purchase him, nor honours, peaceably,
And force were brutish: what a great worth's gone with him,
And but a gentleman! Well, for his sake
I'll ne'er offend more those I cannot make:
They were his words, and shall be dear to memory.
Say I desire to see him once again—
Yet stay, he's so well forward of his peace,
'Twere pity to disturb him: he would groan
Like a soul fetch'd again, and that were injury,
And I've wrong'd his degree too much already.
Call forth the gentlemen of our chamber instantly.

SERVANT within
I shall, my lord.

DUKE
I may forget again,
And therefore will prevent: the strain of this
Troubles me so; one would not hazard more.

[Enter **LA NOVE** and diverse others and the **THREE OTHER GENTLEMEN**.

GENTLEMEN
Your will, my lord?

DUKE
Yes; I discharge you all.

SECOND GENTLEMAN
My lord!

DUKE
Your places shall be otherwise dispos'd of.

FOURTH GENTLEMAN
Why, sir?

DUKE
Reply not, I dismiss you all.
Y'are gentlemen, your worths will find you fortunes;
Nor shall your farewell tax me of ingratitude:
I'll give you all noble remembrances,
As testimonies 'gainst reproach and malice,
That you departed lov'd.

THIRD GENTLEMAN
This is most strange, sir.

LA NOVE
But how is your grace furnish'd, these dismiss'd?

DUKE
Seek me out grooms,
Men more insensible of reputation,
Less curious and precise in terms of honour,
That if my anger chance let fall a stroke,
As we are all subject to impetuous passions,
Yet it may pass unmurmur'd, undisputed,
And not with braver fury prosecuted.

LA NOVE
It shall be done, my lord.

Exit **DUKE**.

THIRD GENTLEMAN
Know you the cause, sir?

LA NOVE
Not I, kind gentlemen, but by conjectures,
And so much shall be yours when you please.

FOURTH GENTLEMAN
Thanks, sir.

THIRD GENTLEMAN
We shall i' th' meantime think ourselves guilty
Of some foul fault, through ignorance committed.

LA NOVE
No, 'tis not that, nor that way.

FOURTH GENTLEMAN
For my part,
I shall be disinherited, I know so much.

LA NOVE
Why, sir, for what?

FOURTH GENTLEMAN
My sire's of a strange humour;
He'll form faults for me, and then swear 'em mine,
And commonly the first begins with lechery.
He knows his own youth's trespass.

LA NOVE
Before you go,
I'll come and take my leave, and tell you all, sirs.

THIRD GENTLEMAN
Thou wert ever just and kind.

LA NOVE
That's my poor virtue, sir,
And parcel valiant, but it's hard to be perfect.

[Exeunt the **THREE OTHER GENTLEMEN**.

The choosing of these fellows now will puzzle me,
Horribly puzzle me, and there's no judgment
Goes true upon man's outside, there's the mischief:
He must be touch'd and try'd for gold or dross.
There is no other way for't, and that's dangerous too;
But since I'm put in trust, I will attempt it:
The duke shall keep one daring man about him.

[Enter a **GALLANT**.

[Aside] Soft, who comes here? A pretty bravery this:
Everyone goes so like a gentleman,

'Tis hard to find a difference but by th' touch.
I'll try your mettle sure.

[Boxes his ear.]

GALLANT
Why, what do you mean, sir?

LA NOVE
Nay, and you understand it not, I do not.

GALLANT
Yes, would you should well know;
I understand it for a box o' th' ear, sir.

LA NOVE
And o' my troth, that's all I gave it for.

GALLANT
'Twere best it be so.

LA NOVE [Aside]
This is a brave coward,
A jolly threat'ning coward; he shall be captain.—
Sir, let me meet you an hour hence i' th' lobby.

GALLANT
Meet you? The world might laugh at me then, i'faith.

LA NOVE
Lay by your scorn and pride, they're scurvy qualities,
And meet me, or I'll box you while I have you,
And carry you gambrell'd thither like a mutton.

GALLANT
Nay, an' you be in earnest, here's my hand
I will not fail you.

LA NOVE
'Tis for your own good.

GALLANT
Away.

LA NOVE
Too much for your own good, sir, a pox on you.

GALLANT

I prithee curse me all day long so.

LA NOVE
Hang you!

GALLANT [Aside]
I'll make him mad; he's loath to curse too much to me.—
Indeed I never yet took box o' th' ear
But it redounded, I must needs say so.

LA NOVE
Will you be gone?

GALLANT
Curse, curse, and then I go.
[Aside] Look how he grins; I've anger'd him to th' kidneys.

[Exit.

LA NOVE
Was ever such a prigging coxcomb seen?
One might have beat him dumb now in this humour,
And he'd ha' grinn'd it out still.

[Enter a **PLAIN FELLOW**.

Oh, here's one
Made to my hand, methinks looks like a craven;
Less pains will serve his trial: some slight justle.

[Justles him.]

PLAIN FELLOW
How!

[Striking him]

Take you that, sir, and if that content you not—

LA NOVE
Yes, very well, sir, I desire no more.

PLAIN FELLOW
I think you need not, for you have not lost by't.

[Exit.

LA NOVE

Who would ha' thought this would have prov'd a gentleman?
I'll never trust long chins and little legs again;
I'll know 'em sure for gentlemen hereafter:
A gristle but in show, but gave his cuff
With such a fetch and reach of gentry,
As if h' had had his arms before the flood.
I have took a villainous hard task upon me;
Now I begin to have a feeling on't.

[Enter **LAPET** carrying a printers' proof and **GALOSHIO** the clown his servant, and so habited.

[Aside] Oh, here comes a try'd piece now, the reformed kick.
The millions of punches, spurns, and nips
That he has endur'd! His buttock's all black lead,
He's half a negro backward; he was past a Spaniard
In eighty-eight, and more Egyptian-like.
His table and his book come both out shortly,
And all the cowards in the town expect it,
So if I fail of my full number now,
I shall be sure to find 'em at church corners,
Where Dives and the suff'ring ballads hang.

LAPET [To **GALOSHIO**]
Well, since thou art of so mild a temper,
Of so meek a spirit, thou mayst live with me
Till better times do smile on thy deserts.
I am glad I am got home again.

GALOSHIO
I am happy
In your service, sir; you'll keep me from the hospital.

LAPET
So, bring me the last proof; this is corrected.

GALOSHIO
Ay, y'are too full of your correction, sir.

LAPET
Look, I have perfect books within this half hour.

GALOSHIO
Yes, sir.

LAPET
Bid him put all the thumps in pica Roman,
And with great T's, you vermin, as thumps should be.

GALOSHIO
Then in what letter will you have your kicks?

LAPET
All in Italica, your backward blows
All in Italica, you hermaphrodite!
When shall I teach you wit?

GALOSHIO [Aside]
Oh, let it alone
Till you have some yourself, sir.

LAPET
You mumble?

GALOSHIO
The victuals are lock'd up; I'm kept from mumbling.

[Exit.

LAPET
He prints my blows upon pot-paper too, the rogue,
Which had been proper for some drunken pamphlet.

LA NOVE
Monsieur Lapet? How the world rings of you, sir!
Your name sounds far and near.

LAPET
A good report
It bears for an enduring name.

LA NOVE
What luck have you, sir!

LAPET
Why, what's the matter?

LA NOVE
I'm but thinking on't.
I've heard you wish this five year for a place:
Now there's one fall'n, and freely without money too;
And empty yet, and yet you cannot have 't.

LAPET
No? What's the reason? I'll give money for't
Rather than go without, sir.

LA NOVE
That's not it, sir;
The troth is, there's no gentleman must have it
Either for love or money: 'tis decreed so;
I was heartily sorry when I thought upon you.
Had you not been a gentleman I had fitted you.

LAPET
Who, I a gentleman? A pox, I'm none, sir.

LA NOVE
How!

LAPET
How? Why, did you ever think I was?

LA NOVE
What? Not a gentleman?

LAPET
I would thou'd'st put it upon me, i'faith.
Did not my grandfather cry coney-skins,
My father aqua vitae? A hot gentleman:
All this I speak on i' your time and memory too;
Only a rich uncle died and left me chattels,
You know all this so well too.

LA NOVE
Pray excuse me, sir,
Ha' not you arms?

LAPET
Yes, a poor couple here
That serve to thrust in wild fowl.

LA NOVE
Herald's arms,
Symbols of gentry, sir: you know my meaning;
They've been shown and seen.

LAPET
They have.

LA NOVE
I'fecks, have they!

LAPET
Why, I confess, at my wife's instigation once,

As women love these heralds' kickshaws naturally,
I bought 'em, but what are they, think you? Puffs.

LA NOVE
Why, that's proper to your name being Lapet,
Which is La Fart, after the English letter.

LAPET
The herald, sir, had much ado to find it.

LA NOVE
And can you blame him?
Why, 'tis the only thing that puzzles the devil.

LAPET
At last he look'd upon my name again,
And having well compar'd it, this he gave me:
The two colics playing upon a wind instrument.

LA NOVE
An excellent proper one. But I pray tell me,
How does he express the colics? They are hard things.

LAPET
The colics? With hot trenchers at their bellies;
There's nothing better, sir, to blaze a colic.

LA NOVE
And are not you a gentleman by this, sir?

LAPET
No, I disclaim 't:
No bellyache upon earth shall make me one;
He shall not think to put his gripes upon me
And wring out gentry so, and ten pound first.
If the wind instrument will make my wife one,
Let her enjoy 't, for she was a harper's grandchild,
But, sir, for my particular, I renounce it.

LA NOVE
Or to be call'd so?

LAPET
Ay, sir, or imagin'd.

LA NOVE
None fitter for the place: give me thy hand.

LAPET
A hundred thousand thanks, beside a bribe, sir.

LA NOVE
You must take heed of thinking toward a gentleman now.

LAPET
Pish, I am not mad, I warrant you. Nay, more, sir,
If one should twit me i' th' teeth that I'm a gentleman,
Twit me their worst, I am but one since Lammas,
That I can prove, if they would see my heart out.

LA NOVE
Marry, in any case keep me that evidence.

[Enter **GALOSHIO** the clown with printers' proofs.

LAPET
Here comes my servant, sir, Galoshio.
H'as not his name for naught, he will be trod upon.
What says my printer now?

GALOSHIO
Here's your last proof, sir.
You shall have perfect books now in a twinkling.

LAPET
These marks are ugly.

GALOSHIO
He says, sir, they're proper:
Blows should have marks, or else they are nothing worth.

LAPET
But why a peel-crow here?

GALOSHIO
I told 'im so, sir:
A scarecrow had been better.

LAPET
How, slave! Look you, sir,
Did not I say this wherret and this bob
Should be both pica Roman?

GALOSHIO
So said I, sir,
Both picked Romans, and he has made 'em Welsh bills;

Indeed I know not what to make on 'em.

LAPET
Heyday! A souse Italica?

GALOSHIO
Yes, that may hold, sir,
Souse is a bona roba, so is flops too.

LAPET
But why stands bastinado so far off here?

GALOSHIO
Alas, you must allow him room to lay about him, sir.

LAPET
Why lies this spurn lower than that spurn, sir?

GALOSHIO
Marry, this signifies one kick'd downstairs, sir,
The other in a gallery. I ask'd him all these questions.

LA NOVE
Your book's name? Prithee, Lapet, mind me,
You never told me yet.

LAPET
Marry, but shall, sir:
'Tis call'd The Uprising of the Kick,
And the Downfall of the Duello.

LA NOVE
Bring that to pass you'll prove a happy member
And do your country service: your young bloods
Will thank you then when they see fourscore.

LAPET
I hope
To save my hundred gentlemen a month by't,
Which will be very good for the private house.

GALOSHIO
Look you, your table's finish'd, sir, already.

LAPET
Why then, behold my masterpiece: see, see, sir,
Here's all your blows and blow-men whatsoever,
Set in their lively colours, givers and takers.

LA NOVE
Troth, wondrous fine, sir.

LAPET
Nay, but mark the postures:
The standing of the takers I admire
More than the givers; they stand scornfully,
Most contumeliously, I like not them.
Oh, here's one cast into a comely figure.

GALOSHIO
My master means him there that's cast down headlong.

LAPET
How sweetly does this fellow take his doust,
Stoops like a camel, that heroic beast,
At a great load of nutmegs! And how meekly
This other fellow here receives his wherret!

GALOSHIO
Oh, master, here's a fellow stands most gallantly,
Taking his kick in private behind the hangings,
And raising up his hips to't! But oh, sir,
How daintily this man lies trampled on!
Would I were in thy place, whate'er thou art.
How lovely he endures it!

LA NOVE
But will not
These things, sir, be hard to practise, think you?

LAPET
Oh, easy, sir: I'll teach 'em in a dance.

LA NOVE
How! In a dance?

LAPET
I'll lose my new place else,
Whate'er it be; I know not what 'tis yet.

LA NOVE
And now you put me in mind, I could employ it well
For your grace specially, for the duke's cousin
Is by this time in's violent fit of mirth,
And a device must be sought out for suddenly
To overcloy the passion.

LAPET
Say no more, sir;
I'll fit you with my scholars, new practitioners,
Endurers of the time.

GALOSHIO
Whereof I am one, sir.

LA NOVE
You carry it away smooth; give me thy hand, sir.

[Exeunt.

ACT V

SCENE I - The Palace

Enter the two **BROTHERS**.

PASSIONATE LORD [Within]
Ha, ha, ha!

SECOND BROTHER
Hark, hark, how loud his fit's grown.

PASSIONATE LORD [Within]
Ha, ha, ha!

FIRST BROTHER
Now let our sister lose no time, but ply it
With all the power she has.

SECOND BROTHER
Her shame grows big, brother;
The Cupid's shape will hardly hold it longer:
'Twould take up half an ell of China damask more,
And all too little, it struts per'lously.
There is no tamp'ring with these Cupids long;
The mere conceit with womankind works strong.

PASSIONATE LORD [Within]
Ha, ha, ha!

SECOND BROTHER
The laugh comes nearer now;

'Twere good we were not seen yet.

[Exeunt **BROTHERS.** Enter **PASSIONATE LORD** and **BASE** his jester.

PASSIONATE LORD
Ha, ha, ha!
And was he bastinado'd to the life?
Ha, ha, ha! I prithee say, lord general,
How did the rascals entrench themselves?

BASE
Most deeply, politicly, all in ditches.

PASSIONATE LORD
Ha, ha, ha!

BASE
'Tis thought he'll ne'er bear arms i' th' field again;
H'as much ado to lift 'em to his head, sir.

PASSIONATE LORD
I would he had.

BASE
On either side round truncheons
Play'd so thick that shoulders, chines, nay, flanks
Were paid to th' quick.

PASSIONATE LORD
Well said, lord general! Ha, ha, ha!

BASE
But pray how grew the difference first betwixt you?

PASSIONATE LORD
There was never any, sir; there lies the jest, man:
Only because he was taller than his brother,
There's all my quarrel to him, and methought
He should be beaten for't; my mind so gave me, sir,
I could not sleep for't. Ha, ha, ha, ha!
Another good jest quickly, while 'tis hot now;
Let me not laugh in vain: ply me, oh, ply me,
As you will answer 't to my cousin duke.

BASE
Alas, who has a good jest?

PASSIONATE LORD

I fall, I dwindle in't.

BASE
Ten crowns for a good jest!

[Enter **SERVANT**.

Ha' you a good jest, sir?

SERVANT
A pretty moral one.

BASE
Let's ha't, whate'er it be.

SERVANT
There comes a Cupid
Drawn by six fools.

[Exit **SERVANT**.

BASE
That's nothing.

PASSIONATE LORD
Help it, help it then.

BASE
I ha' known six hundred fools drawn by a Cupid.

PASSIONATE LORD
Ay, that, that, that's the smarter moral! Ha, ha, ha!
Now I begin to be song-ripe, methinks.

BASE
I'll sing you a pleasant air, sir, before you ebb.

[**Song.**

PASSIONATE LORD
Oh, how my lungs do tickle! Ha, ha, ha!

BASE
Oh, how my lungs do tickle! Ho, ho, ho!

PASSIONATE LORD
Set a sharp jest
Against my breast,

Then how my lungs do tickle
As nightingales
And things in cambric rails
Sing best against a prickle!
Ha, ha, ha, ha!

BASE
Ho, ho, ho, ho, ha!

PASSIONATE LORD
Laugh!

BASE
Laugh!

PASSIONATE LORD
Laugh!

BASE
Laugh!

PASSIONATE LORD
Wide!

BASE
Loud!

PASSIONATE LORD
And vary!

BASE
A smile is for a simpering novice.

PASSIONATE LORD
One that ne'er tasted caviar.

BASE
Nor knows the smack of dear anchovies.

PASSIONATE LORD
Ha, ha, ha, ha, ha!

BASE
Ho, ho, ho, ho, ho!

PASSIONATE LORD
A giggling waiting-wench for me,
That shows her teeth how white they be.

BASE
A thing not fit for gravity,
For theirs are foul and hardly three.

PASSIONATE LORD
Ha, ha, ha!

BASE
Ho, ho, ho!

PASSIONATE LORD
Democritus, thou ancient fleerer,
Now I miss thy laugh, and ha' since.

BASE
There you nam'd the famous jeerer,
That ever jeer'd in Rome or Athens.

PASSIONATE LORD
Ha, ha, ha!

BASE
Ho, ho, ho!

PASSIONATE LORD
How brave lives he that keeps a fool,
Although the rate be deeper!

BASE
But he that is his own fool, sir,
Does live a great deal cheaper.

PASSIONATE LORD
Sure I shall burst, burst, quite break, thou art so witty.

BASE
'Tis rare to break at court, for that belongs to th' city.

PASSIONATE LORD
Ha, ha, my spleen is almost worn to the last laughter!

BASE
Oh, keep a corner for a friend, a jest may come hereafter!

[Enter **LAPET** and **GALOSHIO** clown and **FOUR OTHER FOOLS**, dancing, the **CUPID** leading and bearing his table, and holding it up to **LAPET** at every strain and acting the postures.

[First strain.

LAPET
Twinge all now, twinge, I say!

[Second strain.

Souse upon souse!

[Third strain.

Douses single!

[Fourth strain.

Justle sides!

[Fifth strain.

Knee belly!

[Sixth strain.

Kicksey-buttock!

[Seventh strain.

Down-derry.

[Enter **SOLDIER**, Shamont's brother, his sword drawn.

SOLDIER
Not angry law nor doors of brass shall keep me
From my wrong's expiation; to thy bowels
I return my disgrace, and after turn
My face to any death that can be sentenc'd.

[Stabs the **PASSIOPNATE LORD**, throws down and tramples **LAPET** and **GALOSHIO**, and exits.

BASE
Murder, oh, murder! Stop the murderer there!

LAPET
I am glad he's gone; h'as almost trod my guts out:
Follow him who list for me, I'll ha' no hand in't.

GALOSHIO

Oh, 'twas your luck and mine to be squelch'd, master.
H'as stamp'd my very puddings into pancakes.

CUPID
Oh, brothers, oh, I fear 'tis mortal! Help, oh, help!
I'm made the wretched'st woman by this accident
That ever love beguil'd.

[Enter her **TWO BROTHERS**.

SECOND BROTHER
We are undone, brother,
Our shames are too apparent. Away, receptacle
Of luxury and dishonour! Most unfortunate,
To make thyself but lucky to thy spoil,
After thy sex's manner! Lift him up, brother;
He breathes not to our comfort, he's too wasted
Ever to cheer us more. A chirurgeon, speedily!
Hence, the unhappiest that e'er stepp'd aside!
She'll be a mother before she's known a bride.

CUPID
Thou hadst a most unfortunate conception,
Whate'er thou prov'st to be; in midst of mirth
Comes ruin for a welcome to thy birth.

[Exeunt.

SCENE II - A Field in the Country

Enter **SHAMONT**.

SHAMONT
This is a beautiful life now, privacy
The sweetness and the benefit of essence.
I see there is no man but may make his paradise,
And it is nothing but his love and dotage
Upon the world's foul joys that keeps him out on't,
For he that lives retir'd in mind and spirit
Is still in paradise, and has his innocence,
Partly allow'd for his companion too,
As much as stands with justice. Here no eyes
Shoot their sharp pointed scorns upon my shame;
They know no terms of reputation here,
No punctual limits, or precise dimensions:
Plain downright honesty is all the beauty

And elegancy of life found amongst shepherds,
For knowing nothing nicely or desiring it
Quits many a vexation from the mind,
With which our quainter knowledge does abuse us.
The name of envy is a stranger here,
That dries men's bloods abroad, robs health and rest;
Why, here's no such fury thought on, no, nor falsehood,
That brotherly disease, fellow-like devil,
That plays within our bosom and betrays us.

[Enter **LA NOVE**.

LA NOVE
Oh, are you here?

SHAMONT
La Nove, 'tis strange to see thee.

LA NOVE
I ha' rid one horse to death to find you out, sir.

SHAMONT
I am not to be found of any man
That saw my shame, nor seen long.

LA NOVE
Good, your attention:
You ought to be seen now and found out, sir,
If ever you desire before your ending
To perform one good office, nay, a dear one;
Man's time can hardly match it.

SHAMONT
Be't as precious
As reputation, if it come from court
I will not hear on't.

LA NOVE
You must hear of this, sir.

SHAMONT
Must?

LA NOVE
You shall hear it.

SHAMONT
I love thee, that thou'lt die.

LA NOVE

'Twere nobler in me
Than in you living: you will live a murderer
If you deny this office.

SHAMONT

Ev'n to death, sir.

LA NOVE

Why, then you'll kill your brother.

SHAMONT

How!

LA NOVE

Your brother, sir:
Bear witness, heaven, this man destroys his brother
When he may save him, his least breath may save him.
Can there be wilfuller destruction?
He was forc'd to take a most unmanly wrong,
Above the suff'ring virtue of a soldier,
Has kill'd his injurer, a work of honour,
For which, unless you save him, he dies speedily.
My conscience is discharg'd; I'm but a friend:
A brother should go forward where I end.

[Exit.

SHAMONT

Dies?
Say he be naught, that's nothing to my goodness,
Which ought to shine through use, or else it loses
The glorious name 'tis known by: he's my brother;
Yet peace is above blood. Let him go, ay.
But where's the nobleness of affection then?
That must be car'd for too, or I'm imperfect:
The same blood that stood up in wrath against him
Now in his misery runs all to pity.
I'd rather die than speak one syllable
To save myself, but living as I am,
There's no avoiding on't: the world's humanity
Expects it hourly from me. Curse of fortune,
I took my leave so well too. Let him die,
'Tis but a brother lost; so pleasingly
And swiftly I came off, 'twere more than irksomeness
To tread that path again, and I shall never
Depart so handsomely. But then where's posterity?

The consummation of our house and name?
I'm torn in pieces betwixt love and shame.

[Exit.

SCENE III - The Palace

Enter **LAPET, CLOWN, POLTROT, MOULBAZON,** and **OTHERS,** the new court officers.

LAPET
Good morrow, fellow Poltrot, and Moulbazon,
Good morrow fellows all.

POLTROT
Monsieur Lapet?

LAPET [Giving them books]
Look, I've rememb'red you; here's books apiece for you.

MOULBAZON
Oh, sir, we dearly thank you.

LAPET
So you may;
There's two impressions gone already, sirs.

POLTROT
What? No! In so short a time?

LAPET
'Tis as I tell you, sir;
My Kick sells gallantly, I thank my stars.

GALOSHIO
So does your table; you may thank the moon too.

LAPET
'Tis the book sells the table.

GALOSHIO
But 'tis the bookseller
That has the money for 'em, I'm sure o' that.

LAPET
'Twill much enrich the company of stationers;
'Tis thought 'twill prove a lasting benefit,

Like The Wise Masters, and the almanacs,
The Hundred Novels, and The Book of Cookery,
For they begin already to engross it
And make it a stock-book, thinking indeed
'Twill prove too great a benefit and help
For one that's new set up: they know their way
And make him warden ere his beard be gray.

MOULBAZON
Is't possible such virtue should lie hid,
And in so little paper?

LAPET
How? Why, there was The Carpenter,
An unknown thing, an odoriferous pamphlet,
Yet no more paper, by all computation,
Than Ajax Telamon would use at once;
Your Herring prov'd the like, able to buy
Another Fisher's Folly, and your Pasquill
Went not below the Mad-Caps of that time.
And shall my elaborate Kick come behind, think you?

GALOSHIO
Yes, it must come behind: 'tis in Italica too,
According to your humour.

LAPET
Not in sale, varlet.

GALOSHIO
In sale, sir? It shall sail beyond 'em all, I trow.

LAPET
What have you there now? Oh, page twenty-one.

GALOSHIO
That page is come to his years; he should be a serving-man.

LAPET
Mark how I snap up The Duello there:
One would not use a dog so,
I must needs say, but's for the common good.

GALOSHIO
Nay, sir, your commons seldom fight at sharp,
But buffet in a warehouse.

LAPET

This will save
Many a gentleman of good blood from bleeding, sirs.
I have a curse from many a barber-surgeon;
They'd give but too much money to call 't in.
Turn to page forty-five, see what you find there.

GALOSHIO
Oh, out upon him! Page forty-five: that's an old thief indeed.

[Enter **DUKE**, the **LADY** his sister, **LA NOVE**.

LAPET
The duke! Clap down your books! Away, Galoshio.

GALOSHIO
Indeed I am too foul to be i' th' presence;
They use to shake me off at the chamber door still.

[Exit.

LADY
Good my lord, grant my suit; let me not rise
Without the comfort on't: I have not often
Been tedious in this kind.

DUKE
Sister, you wrong yourself
And those great virtues that your fame is made of
To waste so much breath for a murderer's life.

LADY
You cannot hate th' offense more than I do, sir,
Nor the offender: the respect I owe
Unto his absent brother makes me a suitor,
A most importunate suitor; make me worthy
But of this one request.

DUKE
I am deaf
To any importunacy, and sorry
For your forgetfulness; you never injur'd
Your worth so much, you ought to be rebuk'd for't:
Pursue good ways, end as you did begin;
'Tis half the guilt to speak for such a sin.

LADY
This is love's beggary right that now is ours,
When ladies love and cannot show their powers.

[Exit.

DUKE
La Nove?

LA NOVE
My lord.

DUKE
Are these our new attendants?

LAPET
We are, my lord, and will endure as much
As better men, my lord, and more I trust.

DUKE
What's he?

LA NOVE
My lord, a decay'd gentleman
That will do any service.

DUKE
A decay'd one?

LA NOVE
A renounc'd one indeed, for this place only.

DUKE
We renounce him then; go, discharge him instantly.
He that disclaims his gentry for mere gains,
That man's too base to make a vassal on.

LAPET
What says the duke?

LA NOVE
Faith, little to your comfort, sir:
You must be a gentleman again.

LAPET
How!

LA NOVE
There's no remedy.

LAPET

Marry, the fates forfend! Ne'er while I breathe, sir.

LA NOVE
The duke will have it so, there's no resisting.
He spy'd it i' your forehead.

LAPET
My wife's doing.
She thought she should be put below her betters now,
And sued to ha' me a gentleman again.

LA NOVE
And very likely, sir.
Marry, I'll give you this comfort: when all's done,
You'll never pass but for a scurvy one;
That's all the help you have. Come, show your pace.

LAPET
The heaviest gentleman that e'er lost place;
Bear witness I am forc'd to't.

[Exit with **LA NOVE**.

DUKE
Though you have a coarser title yet upon you
Than those that left your places without blame,
'Tis in your power to make yourselves the same.
I cannot make you gentlemen: that's a work
Rais'd from your own deservings; merit, manners,
And inborn virtue does it. Let your own goodness
Make you so great, my power shall make you greater;
And more t' encourage you, this I add again,
There's many grooms now exact gentlemen.

[Enter **SHAMONT** and stands apart.

SHAMONT
Methinks 'tis strange to me to enter here.
Is there in nature such an awful power
To force me to this place and make me do this?
Is man's affections stronger than his will,
His resolution? Was I not resolv'd
Never to see this place more? Do I bear
Within my breast one blood that confounds th'other,
The blood of love and will, and the last weakest?
Had I ten millions, I would give it all now
I were but past it, or 'twould never come,
For I shall never do't, or not do't well,

But spoil it utterly betwixt two passions.
Yonder's the duke himself; I will not do't now,
Had twenty lives their several sufferings in him.

[Exit.

DUKE
Who's that went out now?

POLTROT
I saw none, my lord.

DUKE
Nor you?

MOULBAZON
I saw the glimpse of one, my lord.

DUKE
Whate'er it was, methought it pleas'd me strangely,
And suddenly my joy was ready for't.
Did you not mark it better?

POLTROT and **MOULBAZON**
Troth, my lord,
We gave no great heed to't.

[Enter **SHAMONT**.

SHAMONT [Aside]
'Twill not be answer'd;
It brings me hither still, by main force hither.
Either I must give over to profess humanity
Or I must speak for him.

DUKE
'Tis here again:
No marvel 'twas so pleasing, 'tis delight
And worth itself, now it appears unclouded.

SHAMONT
My lord—
[Aside] He turns away from me. By this hand,
I am ill-us'd of all sides: 'tis a fault
That fortune ever had t' abuse a goodness.

DUKE
Methought you were saying somewhat.

SHAMONT [Aside]
Mark the language,
As coy as fate; I see 'twill ne'er be granted.

DUKE
We little look'd in troth to see you here yet.

SHAMONT [Aside]
Not till the day after my brother's death, I think.

DUKE
Sure some great business drew you.

SHAMONT
No, in sooth, sir,
Only to come to see a brother die, sir,
That I may learn to go too; and if he deceive me not,
I think he will do well in't of a soldier,
Manly and honestly: and if he weep then,
I shall not think the worse on's manhood for't,
Because he's leaving of that part that has it.

DUKE
H'as slain a noble gentleman, think on't, sir!

SHAMONT
I would I could not, sir.

DUKE
Our kinsman too.

SHAMONT
All this is but worse, sir.

DUKE
When 'tis at worst,
Yet seeing thee, he lives.

SHAMONT
My lord!

DUKE
He lives;
Believe it as thy bliss, he dies not for't.
Will this make satisfaction for things past?

SHAMONT [Kneeling]

Oh, my lord!

DUKE
Will it? Speak.

SHAMONT
With greater shame to my unworthiness.

DUKE
Rise then, we're ev'n. I never found it harder
To keep just with a man; my great work's ended.
I knew your brother's pardon was your suit, sir,
However your nice modesty held it back.

SHAMONT
I take a joy now to confess it, sir.

[Enter **LA NOVE**.

LA NOVE
My lord—

DUKE
Hear me first, sir, whate'er your news be:
Set free the soldier instantly.

LA NOVE
'Tis done, my lord.

DUKE
How!

LA NOVE
In effect: 'twas part of my news too;
There's fair hope of your noble kinsman's life, sir.

DUKE
What sayst thou?

LA NOVE
And the most admired change
That living flesh e'er had. He's not the man, my lord;
Death cannot be more free from passions, sir,
Than he is at this instant: he's so meek now,
He makes those seem passionate were never thought of,
And for he fears his moods have oft disturb'd you, sir,
He's only hasty now for his forgiveness;
And here behold him, sir.

[Enter **PASSIONATE LORD**, the **CUPID**, and her **TWO BROTHERS**.

DUKE
Let me give thanks first.
Our worthy cousin.

PASSIONATE LORD
Your unworthy trouble, sir,
For which, with all acknowledg'd reverence,
I ask your pardon; and for injury
More known and willful, I have chose a wife
Without your counsel or consent, my lord.

DUKE
A wife? Where is she, sir?

PASSIONATE LORD
This noble gentlewoman.

DUKE
How!

PASSIONATE LORD
Whose honour my forgetful times much wrong'd.

DUKE
He's madder than he was.

LA NOVE
I would ha' sworn for him.

DUKE
The Cupid, cousin?

PASSIONATE LORD
Yes, this worthy lady, sir.

DUKE
Still worse and worse.

FIRST BROTHER
Our sister, under pardon, my lord.

DUKE
What?

SECOND BROTHER

Which shape love taught her to assume.

DUKE
Is't truth then?

LA NOVE
It appears plainly now below the waist, my lord.

DUKE
Shamont, didst ever read of a she-Cupid?

SHAMONT
Never in fiction yet, but it might hold, sir,
For desire is of both genders.

[Enter the **LADY**, the Duke's sister.

DUKE
Make that good here:
I take thee at thy word, sir.

[He joins **SHAMONT'S HAND** and his **SISTER'S**.

SHAMONT
Oh, my lord,
Love would appear too bold and rude from me:
Honour and admiration are her rights;
Her goodness is my saint, my lord.

DUKE
I see
Y'are both too modest to bestow yourselves:
I'll save that virtue still; 'tis but my pains.
Come, it shall be so.

SHAMONT
This gift does but set forth my poverty.

LADY
Sir, that which you complain of is my riches.

[Enter Shamont's brother the **SOLDIER**.

DUKE
Soldier, now every noise sounds peace, th'art welcome.

SOLDIER [Kneeling]
Sir, my repentance sues for your bless'd favour,

Which once obtain'd no injury shall lose it;
I'll suffer mightier wrongs.

DUKE
Rise, lov'd and pardon'd,
For where hope fail'd, nay, art itself resign'd;
Thou'st wrought that cure, which skill could never find,
Nor did there cease, but to our peace extend:
Never could wrongs boast of a nobler end.

[Exeunt.

THE EPILOGUE

Our poet bid us say, for his own part,
He cannot lay too much forth of his art,
But fears our overacting passions may,
As not adorn, deface his labour'd play:
Yet still he is resolute for what is writ
Of nicer valour, and assumes the wit.
But for the love-scenes, which he ever meant
Cupid in's petticoat should represent,
He'll stand no shock of censure; the play's good,
He says he knows it, if well understood.
But we, blind god, beg, if thou art divine,
Thou'lt shoot thy arrows round, this play was thine.

Thomas Middleton – A Short Biography

Thomas Middleton was born in London in April 1580 and baptised on 18th April. He was the son of a bricklayer who had raised himself to the status of a gentleman and become the owner of property adjoining the Curtain Theatre in Shoreditch.

Middleton was aged only five when his father died. His mother remarried but this new union unfortunately fell apart and turned into a fifteen year legal conflict centered on the inheritance of Thomas and his younger sister.

Middleton went on to attend Queen's College, Oxford, matriculating in 1598. However he failed to graduate for reasons unknown leaving either in 1600 or 1601. He had by that time written and published three long poems in popular Elizabethan styles. None appears to have been commercially successful although Microcynicon: Six Snarling Satirese was denounced by the Archbishop of Canterbury and publicly burned as part of his attack on verse satire. Although a minor work, the poems show the roots of Middleton's interest in, and later mature work on, sin, hypocrisy, and lust.

In the early years of the 17th century, Middleton made a living writing topical pamphlets, including one, Penniless Parliament of Threadbare Poets, that was reprinted several times as well as becoming the subject of a parliamentary inquiry.

For one so young he was already making quite an impact and had obviously attracted the eye of the authorities in those turbulent times.

Records surviving of the great theatrical entrepreneur of the day, Philip Henslowe, confirm that Middleton was writing for Henslowe's Admiral's Men. His lauded contemporary, a certain William Shakespeare, was writing only for Henslowe whereas Middleton remained a free agent and able to write for whichever theatrical company hired him.

These early years writing plays continued to attract controversy. His friendship and writing partnership with Thomas Dekker brought him into conflict with Ben Jonson and George Chapman in the so-called War of the Theatres. (This controversy was also called the Poetomachia by Thomas Dekker. The Bishops Ban of 1599 had removed any use of satire from prose and verse publications and so the only outlet was on the stage. For the next 3 years Ben Jonson and George Chapman on one side and John Marston, Thomas Dekker and Thomas Middleton on the other poked fun at their opposition with characters from their plays. The grudge against Jonson continued as late as 1626, when Jonson's play The Staple of News indulges in a slur on Middleton's last play, A Game at Chess).

In 1603, Middleton married. It was also a momentous year in other respects. On the death of Elizabeth I, her cousin James VI of Scotland was now also crowned King James I of England. Another outbreak of the plague now forced the theatres in London to close.

For Middleton the changeover from Elizabethan to Jacobean was the beginning of a long period of success as a writer.

When the theatres re-opened and welcomed back audiences in need of entertainment Middleton was there, writing for several different companies. In particular he specialised in city comedy and revenge tragedy.

During this time he appears also to have written with Shakespeare and he is variously attributed as collaborating on All's Well That Ends Well and Timon of Athens.

Although Middleton had started as a junior partner to Thomas Dekker he was now his fully fledged equal. His finest work with Dekker was undoubtedly The Roaring Girl, a biography of the notorious contemporary thief Mary Frith (Frith began her criminal career as a pickpocket before moving on to highway robbery with a penchant for dressing up as a man. A spell in prison was followed by a long career as a 'fence' from her shop in Fleet St. She lived to the then quite extraordinary age of 74.) The writing is noteworthy not only for its playwriting ambition but in producing a fully formed heroine in Moll Cutpurse. This was only shortly after the role of women in plays had seen fit to have them played, in the main, by men.

In the 1610s, Middleton began another playwriting partnership, this time with the actor William Rowley, producing another slew of plays including the classics Wit at Several Weapons and A Fair Quarrel.

The ever adaptable Middleton seemed at ease working with others or by himself. His solo writing credits include the comic masterpiece, A Chaste Maid in Cheapside, in 1613. Interestingly his solo plays are somewhat less thrusting and bellicose. Certainly there is no comedy among them with the satirical depth of Michaelmas Term and no tragedy as raw, striking and as bloodthirsty as The Revenger's Tragedy.

There may be various reasons for this and among them that he was increasingly involved with civic pageants and therefore was trying to avoid too much controversy especially without the cover of a collaborator. Indeed in 1620, he was officially appointed as chronologer of the City of London, a post he held until his death in 1627, when ironically, it passed to his great rival, and sometime enemy, Ben Jonson.

Middleton's official duties did not interrupt his dramatic writing; the 1620s saw the production of his and Rowley's tragedy, and continual favourite, The Changeling, as well as several other tragicomedies.

However in 1624, he reached a peak of notoriety when his dramatic allegory A Game at Chess was staged by the King's Men. The play used the conceit of a chess game to present and satirise the recent intrigues surrounding the Spanish Match; James I's son, Prince Charles, was being positioned to marry the daughter, Maria Anna of the Spanish King Philip IV of Spain. Though Middleton's approach was strongly patriotic, the Privy Council closed the play, after only nine performances at the Globe theatre, having received a complaint from the Spanish ambassador. The Privy Council then opened a prosecution against both authors and actors. Although Middleton in his defence showed that the play had been passed by the Master of the Revels, Sir Henry Herbert, any further performance was forbidden and the author and actors fined.

What happened next is a mystery. It is the last play recorded as having being written by Middleton. His playwriting career appears to have stopped dead. It follows that some sort of further punishment probably occurred and for a writer can there be any greater punishment than not being allowed to write or be heard?

Middleton's work is diverse even by the standards of his age. His career Middleton covers many many genres including tragedy, history and city comedy. As we have noted he did not have the kind of official relationship with a particular company that Shakespeare or Fletcher had that might have supported him in a lean creative period. Instead he appears to have written on a freelance basis for any number of companies. His output ranges from the "snarling" satire of Michaelmas Term, performed by the Children of Paul's, to the bleak intrigues of The Revenger's Tragedy, performed by the King's Men. Interestingly earlier editions of The Revenger's Tragedy attributed the play solely to Cyril Tourneur but recent studies have shredded that view so that Middleton's authorship is not now seriously contested

Indeed modern techniques in analysing writing styles are now leaning towards giving Middleton credit for his adaptation and revision of Shakespeare's Macbeth and Measure for Measure. Along with the more established evidence of collaboration on All's Well That Ends Well and Timon of Athens it appears that Middleton has moved some way forward to the front rank of playwrights and an association, in some form, but its greatest exponent.

His early work was informed by the blossoming, in the late Elizabethan period, of satire, while his maturity was influenced by the ascendancy of Fletcherian tragicomedy. Middleton's later work, in which his satirical fury is tempered and broadened, includes three of his acknowledged masterpieces. A Chaste

Maid in Cheapside, produced by the Lady Elizabeth's Men, which skillfully combines London life with an expansive view of the power of love to effect reconciliation even though London seems populated entirely by sinners, in which no social rank goes unsatirised. The Changeling, a later tragedy, returns Middleton to an Italianate setting like that of The Revenger's Tragedy, except that here the central characters are more fully drawn and more compelling as individuals. Similar development can be seen in Women Beware Women.

Middleton's plays are marked by their cynicism, though often very funny, about the human race. His characters are complex. True heroes are a rarity: almost all of his characters are selfish, greedy, and self-absorbed.

When Middleton does portray good people, the characters are often presented as flawless and perfect and given small, undemanding roles. A theological pamphlet attributed to Middleton gives sustenance to the notion that Middleton was a strong believer in Calvinism.

Thomas Middleton died at his home at Newington Butts in Southwark in the summer of 1627, and was buried on July 4th, in St Mary's churchyard which today survives as a public park in Elephant and Castle.

Middleton stands with John Fletcher and Ben Jonson as the most successful and prolific of playwrights from the Jacobean period. Very few Renaissance dramatists would achieve equal success in both comedy and tragedy but Middleton was one. He also wrote many masques and pageants and remains, to this day, one of the most notable of Jacobean dramatists.

Middleton's work has long been praised by many literary critics, among the most fervent were Algernon Charles Swinburne and T. S. Eliot. The latter thought Middleton was second only to Shakespeare.

Among their contemporaries was a very crowded field of talent including: Ben Jonson (1572-1637), Christopher Marlowe (1564-1593), Francis Beaumont (1585-1616), Henry Chettle (1564-1606), John Fletcher (1579–1625), John Ford (1586–1639), John Day (1574-1640), John Marston (1576-1634), John Webster (1580-1634), Nathan Field (1587-1620), Philip Massinger (1584-1640), Richard Burbage (1567-1619), Robert Greene (1558-1592), Thomas Dekker (1575-1625), Thomas Kyd (1558-1594), William Haughton (died 1605), William Rowley (1585-1626).

It's a daunting list and confirms that to top that made you a very special talent indeed.

Thomas Middleton – A Concise Bibliography

It has long been recognised that the modern concept of authorship was rather more elastic in centuries past. Writers were not only for hire, and their work therefore a commodity, but their plays ran much shorter lengths; two weeks being a common term of performance. To that themes and scenes were liberally excised from one play and used in another. Revisions to past plays that were being restaged would be undertaken and entirely credited to other writers. Many works and plays were unpublished and have not survived and some only from memory by actors etc. Whilst many of these playwrights are only now feted for their talents, some undoubtedly were at the time, but it is difficult to, in every case, to establish exact provenance. With modern scholarly and literary techniques author attributions have sometimes changed or been re-balanced. For those where this may be the case we have placed the *Play's Title and other information* in italics

www.ingramcontent.com/pod-product-compliance
Lightning Source LLC
Chambersburg PA
CBHW060139050426
42448CB00010B/2202